W9-CYU-403

CHAPTER 1

Information Literacy for an Information Generation

The second graders were intrigued as I read about how and why birds build nests, especially weaverbirds. They wanted to know why the weaverbird's nest is shaped so oddly and how the bird gets into the nest with the long, funnel-shaped entrance. "So where can we find out?" I asked the group. In unison, the class responded, "The Internet!" Ask almost any student these days where to find information on any topic and "the Internet" is usually his or her answer.

We live in a world of information that is readily accessible. Rather than go to the library to find information in books, we carry libraries on our laptops. With the press of a key we can find the location of Lithuania, the temperature in Taiwan, or the size of the Seychelles.

In fact, children born since the early eighties have been dubbed the Net Generation (Tapscott, 1999)—or, as I refer to it, the Information Generation because technology and the information it supplies is a natural part of their daily lives. For them, finding information on the Internet is as simple as tying their shoe. They "Google" a telephone number rather than consult a traditional directory. They go to a cinema's Web site rather than the newspaper to find out movie times. They check the Internet first for almost any kind of information they seek.

However, growing up with information that is readily available does not ensure that children know what to do with the information once they find it. Take Miles, for example, a typical third grader with a report to write on the Great Basin. After searching the Internet, he downloaded information on the Great Basin and printed it out—all 27 pages. Then he shouted to his mom, "I'm finished." Access to the information did not ensure learning.

Miles is like so many Information Generation students who believe locating information is the end itself and not a means to an end. Little did he realize that he had just begun the process of writing a report. Miles needed *information literacy*, the ability to access, evaluate, and use information effectively (*Information Literacy Standards for Student Learning*, 1998). Whether they find facts from the Internet, a textbook, an article, or reference books, students today need to know how to think about facts and transform them into understanding.

Consider Joshua, an information-literate first grader. After perusing a nonfiction trade book on spiders during recess, he burst through the classroom door, eager to share all he had learned with me. "You won't believe what I learned about spiders!" he exclaimed. "Did you know that spiders do all kinds of cool stuff that you don't think that spiders do? Some can swim and jump and one can even build a trapdoor! I was looking during recess to see what kinds of spiders we got here at school." Clearly, Joshua was thinking about the information as he was reading. He connected the text to what he already knew about spiders, realizing that not all spiders act, move, and spin webs in the same way. He was amazed at how some spiders behave like other animals. "I wonder if they can swim like a fish. Do you think they can jump as high as rabbits?" Then he wanted to take his new understanding and apply it by investigating the playground to see what kinds of spiders live there. And he was eager to share his understanding. Joshua is an Information Generation student who knew how to access, evaluate, and use information effectively.

This book is for teachers and administrators who want to help primary students more effectively read the fact-filled texts they encounter daily—and write those texts themselves. It emphasizes the role that literacy plays in accessing, evaluating, and using information. It helps you apply research-based, classroom-proven practices to develop information-literate students, suggesting ways for using nonfiction text more frequently and wisely in grades K–3.

In this chapter, I argue that our students must be information literate to function in today's classroom and today's world. From there, I show how information literacy applies to our elementary classrooms. Then I discuss the best methods to teach the Information Generation in our elementary classrooms, particularly K–3.

Technology and the Information Generation

As previously stated, technology is the way of life for children today. My son, Brandon, is a perfect example. When I walk into his bedroom, I usually find him sitting at his computer, instant-messaging friends. At the same time, he is texting on his cell phone to other friends, his iPod peeking from his shirt pocket and his Xbox prominently displayed in the background (wired into four other game players across the globe). I survey the scene and ask with astonishment, "What are you doing?!" He looks at me and replies, "My homework, Mom. What does it look like?" And sure enough, there on the desk is his open algebra book, notebook, and pencil. By growing up digital, Brandon has learned to multitask. The new studies about this generation assure me that he really *is* capable of doing his homework while doing all the other things at the same time! (Prensky, 2001b; Roberts, Foehr, Rideout, & Brodie, 2005; Tapscott, 1999).

However, Richard Wurman warns that technology overload can also lead to "information anxiety." The sheer amount of information we confront on a *daily basis* is more than most people confronted in an *entire lifetime* just over 100 years ago. In fact, there has been more information produced in the past 30 years than in the previous 5,000. Information is being produced at such a rapid rate that this information supply is expected to double about every two years (Wurman, Liefer, Sume, & Whitehouse, 2000).

It is the availability and accessibility to so much information that has created new expectations for literacy that impact our schools and classrooms.

Information and Literacy

D ealing with information is essential in today's world (Hammer, 1997; Senge et al., 2000; Wurman et al., 2000). To be successfully employed today, we must know how to determine the information we need, how to find it, and how to apply it to achieve our goals. We must decide what to do with the information and how to share that information with others. The twenty-first-century workplace demands information-literate employees (Braunger & Lewis, 1997; Hammer, 1997; Senge et al., 2000; Tapscott, 1999).

In the last century, reading and writing about facts was deemed sufficient. In this century, we must also think critically about facts to create understanding based on them. This requires a new kind of literacy—a different way of comprehending and using information.

> "Information literacy is a survival skill in the Information Age. Instead of drowning in the abundance of information that floods their lives, information literate people know how to access, evaluate, and use information effectively to solve a particular problem or make a decision—whether the information they select comes from a computer, a book, a government agency, a film or any number of other possible resources."
>
> —*Presidential Committee Report on Information Literacy, 1989*

Today's literacy expectations demand higher levels of thinking about text.

Numerous reports, recommendations, and standards at the national and state levels underscore the importance of thinking about, understanding, and using written information effectively. They point in the direction of information literacy, asking if our students are prepared.

The National Assessment of Education Progress (NAEP) is a government agency that monitors education at the national level. It outlines literacy expectations that emphasize the importance of inferential and critical thinking to develop understanding of text while "thinking about the text" (*Reading Framework for the 2003 National Assessment of Educational Progress*, 2003).

The National Reading Panel (*Report of the National Reading Panel*, 2000) defined comprehension, a critical aspect of literacy, as "creating understanding with cognitive processes requiring intentional thinking," citing the *Literacy Dictionary's* (Harris & Hodges, 1995) definition: "intentional thinking during which meaning is constructed through interactions between text and reader."

The 2003 report from the National Commission on Writing reflects the demands of the new literacy, too. It states that the majority of elementary students' writing nationwide reflected thinking at the literal level and needed to go beyond that: "Educational reform must be expanded to include ideas; the ability of students to think, reason, and communicate" (*The Neglected "R,"* 2003). Writing facts is no longer sufficient—writing must reflect thinking about the information.

To provide our students with access to all this information without the necessary skills for handling it is like throwing students out to sea without a life preserver. We cannot continue teaching students to read and write information at the literal levels as we did in the last century and expect them to know how to think critically and create understanding. We are assessing a new literacy today: information literacy for an Information Generation.

Information Literacy in Primary Classrooms

Why promote information literacy in the primary grades? Shouldn't that be left to the upper-grade teachers? In the early grades we teach students to "learn to read," and then in the upper grades they usually teach them to "read to learn," right?

Wrong. In today's classroom, students are expected to know how to create understanding from nonfiction at proficient levels by fourth grade (*Reading Framework*, 2003). These expectations require students to evaluate information beyond the fact level: to consider the relationships of concepts inside the text and outside the text, to think about the information at a conceptual level, and to put that thinking into writing. Students must be able to *access, evaluate,* and *use* the information.

However, less than 25 percent of our fourth-grade students nationwide were reading at proficient levels according to our latest NAEP reports (2005). It is in grades K–3 that the groundwork must be laid for understanding how nonfiction works.

Our job is to teach our primary students how to read—and that includes reading information. And perhaps we can use more of our large blocks of literacy-instruction time to develop the thinking required of information literacy.

The Information Literacy Standards for Student Learning (1998) are a road map that I use in classrooms to guide instruction. They are national goals, established by the American Association of School Librarians and the Association for Educational Communications and Technology. In this section, I give an overview of each standard as interpreted for the primary classroom. Then, in the following chapters, I share strategies to develop the thinking skills that help students meet these standards.

National Standards for Information Literacy

Standard One: The student who is information literate **accesses information** efficiently and effectively.

Standard Two: The student who is information literate **evaluates information** critically and competently.

Standard Three: The student who is information literate **uses information** accurately and creatively.

Standard One: The Student Who Is Information Literate Accesses Information Efficiently and Effectively

There has been a growing interest in nonfiction in the elementary classrooms in the last few years. Schools are ordering more nonfiction. Book companies are publishing nonfiction for emergent readers. Teachers are using more informational trade books in instruction. So we need to make sure that our young students are learning how to access the information in those texts efficiently and effectively.

Accessing information goes beyond just locating the information in the text. It requires pulling out the information we need to meet our purpose for reading. For example, if we can't figure out how to work our car alarm, we don't read the entire owner's manual to educate ourselves. Instead, we find the section on the car's security system and pull out the information we need.

When I was in the classroom full-time, I made sure my students had *access to information books* during thematic units. I provided books about frogs, weather, and ecology spread out across the chalkboard and in literacy centers. However, when thinking back, I realize that I had not taught my young students *how to access the information within the books.* Instead of teaching students how nonfiction works, I, like so many teachers, spent literacy instruction time teaching them how stories work.

A look around our classrooms paints a pretty clear picture of how most young children learn to read. We read aloud stories to help students learn story structure. They learn that stories have characters, setting, and a problem that the characters try to resolve during the story. Books are read from beginning to end. Literacy instruction is explicit. Students are grouped for varying levels of support. In the early grades of school, children are immersed almost exclusively in fiction (Duke, 2000; Fisher & Hiebert, 1990; Venezky, 2000).

Compare that to the two- to three-minute average per day of literacy instruction with nonfiction text in many first-grade classrooms, or the classrooms in which no literacy instruction with nonfiction was found (Duke, 2000). Teachers often assume that once children learn to read stories, they easily transfer the necessary skills to nonfiction. But that is not necessarily the case (Chall, Jacobs, & Baldwin, 1996).

Different kinds of text demand different kinds of reading strategies. For students to access information efficiently and effectively they must know how nonfiction text works. The strategies explained in this book will help make these differences explicit to young students.

Teaching the Information Generation

Standard Two: The Student Who Is Information Literate Evaluates Information Critically and Competently

Evaluating information is not the same as reading or even memorizing information to recall facts. It is thinking critically about the information (Doyle, 1996; Elder & Paul, 2003; Facione, 2006). Specifically, as the reader thinks about the facts, he considers what he already knows about the topic, what experiences he has had related to it, and how the information connects to other information (Kintsch, 1998; Pearson & Fielding, 1991), like Joshua, whose story was told at the beginning of the chapter. As he analyzes, reasons, interprets, connects, and draws conclusions from the information, he creates understanding.

Facts per se are static. However, the reader's understanding is dynamic and variable—depending on his or her prior knowledge, experiences, beliefs, and thinking habits. For example, in one class I observed all first-grade students were reading the same text about reptiles. The facts were static. However, each child's understanding of those facts was dynamic. As Sam read, he compared the snake in the text to the snake he saw on his camping trip. Johnny, though, was so bogged down in the reading process that he only got pieces of what the text was about. And Lindsay was "grossed out" by a photo in the book and didn't remember any of the facts she read. The following chapters describe strategies to teach young readers to evaluate informational text for understanding.

These second graders are learning to evaluate text about animal teeth.

Standard Three: The Student Who Is Information Literate Uses Information Accurately and Creatively

From state reading exams in the third grade to the SAT in high school, students must not only know how to think critically about information but also how to use it. As Vito Perrone writes, "Our students need to be able to use knowledge, not just know about things" (1994).

In classrooms, we commonly ask students to use information by writing about it, whether in journals, learning logs, retellings, test questions, or reports. Writing about information not only builds children's literacy skills, but also provides us with a powerful, authentic way to assess their learning. When students can write well about information, chances are they understand that information.

And yet, how many of us have sat and listened to children's strained reading of their written reports? As they stumble through their own text, we must question their understanding of the report's content. Most of these students learned about using information by being what Jamie McKenzie (1996) calls "word movers." They have rearranged words from a published sentence or sentences in a published paragraph and called it paraphrasing. Unfortunately, these students do not understand the concepts they are writing about. They have not successfully accessed or evaluated the information.

When students share their understanding in writing, the piece should reflect their ability to organize the information, integrate the information into their prior knowledge, and apply their critical thinking—students should be able to write "accurately and creatively."

Writing must reflect accurate understanding of the content. It must also reflect evidence of creating—of students shaping the new information into their own understanding and then communicating that understanding. To accomplish this, students need explicit teaching of writing *and* thinking. The strategies in this book provide practical ways to teach students how to develop thinking to create understanding and then how to write from that understanding.

Teaching the Information Generation to Think About and Understand Fact-Filled Texts

According to Marc Prensky (2001a), "In a very short time, technology has changed an entire generation's behavior radically, and it behooves all of us who are not from the generation but whose life involves interactions with them, such as parents and teachers, to learn as much as we can about the new behaviors" (p. 13). And he is right. Recognizing these behaviors helps us to address them effectively as we navigate the high expectations for literacy in the twenty-first century. It also helps us to better understand this generation at home and at school.

Take third grader Jeffrey, for example. In a conference with his teacher, his mother describes him this way: "Jeffrey is the most curious kid I know. He is so eager to learn about everything, it seems. He spends hours on the Internet looking up all kinds of stuff. He can tell me about every kind of shark and in what ocean they live. He knows which kinds are aggressive and which aren't. He knows that the smallest one is about the size of your shoe and that the largest is half the size of a football field. You should see what Jeffrey created the other day. He had downloaded some clips about sharks and made his own slide show." However, Jeffrey's teacher describes him this way: "Uninterested and unmotivated, has a difficult time in content areas, doesn't know how to answer questions." Listening in on this conference made me feel there were two Jeffreys: a world Jeffrey and a school Jeffrey.

Jeffrey represents a breed of student that I see all too often these days: the student who knows how to succeed with technology and information outside school, but struggles with text and information in school. These students tend to have more practice and immersion with technology than with texts. Recent research (Roberts et al., 2005) reveals that students spend an average of 6.5 hours per day engaged with some type of electronic media—and squeeze 8.5 hours into those 6.5 hours by multitasking with several types of media (Roberts et al., 2005). Before these students go off to college, it is estimated they will spend over 10,000 hours playing video games, watch over 20,000 hours of television, talk more than 10,000 hours on cell phones, but spend less than 5,000 hours reading (Prensky, 2001b).

Because of growing up digital and their immersion in technology, the Information Generation has developed the following common thinking patterns. It:

- Likes to receive information fast
- Multitasks and parallel processes
- Prefers random access of information
- Prefers graphics to text
- Craves interactivity
- Functions best when networked
  (Prensky, 2001b; Roberts et al., 2005; Tapscott, 1999)

Let's consider how these common thinking behaviors impact learning from text and even interfere with today's higher literacy expectations. See chart on the next page.

Our Information Generation kids come from homes that have an average of:

→ 3.5 TVs

→ 3.3 radios

→ 2.9 VCR/DVD players

→ 1.5 computers

→ 3.6 CD/tape players

24% had 5+ TVs

53% had 3+ VCR/ DVD players

56% owned 2+ game players

34% had DVRs

80% had cable/ satellite TV

63% said the TV is on during meals

68% have TVs in their bedrooms

(Roberts et al., 2005)

Information Generation Thinking Behaviors	Impact on Learning From Text	NAEP-Proficient Reader Expectations
• multitasks and parallel processes	• difficulty focusing attention	• summarize and identify author's intent
• prefers random access of information	• difficulty organizing thinking and looking for relationships within information	• recognize relationships within text • draw reasonable conclusions from text
• prefers graphics to text	• cannot visualize • trouble putting thinking into language	• written response reflecting thinking
• craves interactivity	• does not work well independently without immediate feedback	• interact with text to make connections, inferences, and draw conclusions
• functions best when networked	• needs to talk through thinking to figure out thinking	• metacognitive processing • reflection on learning

Common Information Generation thinking behaviors that can impact learning from fact-filled texts.

Students arrive in our classrooms with scattered energies, accustomed to accessing information at "twitch speeds" (Prensky, 2006). To be a proficient reader, however, a student must focus on what is important in the text, not randomly pull out facts.

They need to develop common thinking behaviors for text that include the following:

- Focusing attention
- Organizing thinking to see relationships
- Visualizing images from text
- Putting thinking into language (orally and written)
- Talking through their thinking
- Reflecting on learning and thinking

Information Generation students must develop cognitive strategies to help them create understanding from text at levels of proficiency demanded by today's literacy expectations.

The focus of this book is on the cognitive strategies necessary for primary students to become information literate. I have chosen six strategies that will develop thinking skills before, during, and after reading information to create understanding: *predicting information, developing vocabulary,*

Many young children have already developed thinking patterns by using technology that is common to the Information Generation.

identifying facts in the text, interpreting facts, making connections to facts, and organizing facts. In Chapters 3 through 7, I show you how to introduce the strategies, model them, and guide students in practicing and applying them. By following my advice, you will help your students learn how to evaluate information at literal, critical, and conceptual levels of understanding, moving them toward being more proficient readers as outlined by NAEP.

Closing Thoughts

Our young students arrive on our doorstep in the primary grades as Information Generation students. Just the other day, my 2-year-old granddaughter told her mother, "Emmie need e-mail." And she crawled into her mother's lap to see what message was on the computer for her! By the time children come to school, they have been immersed in technology from birth and have already adapted many of the thinking patterns of this generation. However, they also arrive with wonder and curiosity as motivated learners, trusting us as teachers to show them the world of learning. We can seize this golden opportunity to capture this innate curiosity and motivation and to open the world of fact-filled texts to these young readers.

CHAPTER 2

Creating Understanding With Nonfiction:
Laying a Theoretical Foundation

Sean was sharing his book about space with the rest of his first-grade class during show-and-tell. "First I went to the table of contents. I was trying to find something, but I couldn't find it."

"What were you trying to find?" asked Meredith, a classmate.

"My favoritest part was a close-up of the spaceship. I couldn't find it so I found something else. I went to 'Stars' and it's telling me page 36." As Sean continued to share, a conversation developed between him, his classmates, and their teacher, Beth Laine.

BETH:	So what did you find, Sean?
SEAN:	Well, it has a life cycle of stars.
BETH	[to the rest of the class]: Did you know stars have a life cycle? Can you tell us about it?

Sean shared what he learned about how stars are "born" and how they "die." As he finished, Margo, another classmate, chimed in.

MARGO:	Look, it's like a circle story. See how it goes back to the beginning.
BETH:	What makes you say that, Margo?
MARGO:	Because it says the star is born, then dies, then is reborn.
BETH:	So you are saying that order matters with this information? [directing the children's attention to an assortment of graphic organizers on the wall] So which plan would you use up there?
CHRIS:	A cyclical or circle one.

BETH:	Good job! [turning to the whole class] Which other one might you use?
SEAN:	For the life cycle you could use this one [pointing to a concept web].
BETH:	That's a concept web. Does order matter in a concept web? Could we use that one?
CHLOE:	No! Order matters when it's born and dies. First it's born, *then* it dies.
MATT:	It tells about the star from beginning to end.
SEAN:	But you can tell about the sun and the moon and the stars.
BETH:	So you are also looking at the information on this side of the page, huh, Sean? You are saying that with this information about the sun and the moon and stars that order doesn't matter.
SEAN:	Right. You can tell about those in any order. It's just a list of facts.
ISAAC:	Today, when we went to the book fair, I found a book on space, and I bought it and I looked at it and it has stars and astronauts and things. So can I bring it tomorrow?

These first graders have learned how to create understanding with nonfiction. They know how to think about the information in the text while thinking about their thinking (which information is related, how it is related, and how it relates to them). They also know a lot about how nonfiction works (how to find the information with the table of contents, how to use the photos, and so forth). And they make their understanding clear to Beth and one another by talking.

Proficient readers do more than think about the facts (content knowledge). They also think about their own thinking (metacognition) and about how the text

Second graders talk through their thinking while reading about spiders.

works (text knowledge) (Jones, Palinscar, Ogle, & Carr, 1987). They interact with the text as they read, making connections to other texts, their lives, and the world, and take away what's most relevant based on those connections. That's why an entire class can read the same set of facts, yet each student's understanding of the facts varies.

J. K. Rowling, author of the Harry Potter series, offers insight into this process. When asked about a movie adaptation of one of her books in an interview (*Newsweek*, June 30, 2003), she replied, "Obviously, I prefer books. I'm a writer. That's always going to be so. The thing about film is that everyone sees the same thing, and that's what will always make it substandard to the novel. Readers have to work with me to create a new Hogwarts every single time every book is read."

Her point is clear: Whether we pick up fiction or nonfiction, reading is a collaborative act between the reader and the text to create understanding. Creating Hogwarts requires work on both the author's and the reader's part. And my Hogwarts will look different from yours. Understanding is individual.

At the same time, especially when it comes to nonfiction, it is important for the reader to *share meaning* with the author—to work *with* the author to create understanding. Why? To ensure that the information he gleans from the text is complete and his understanding of it is accurate. Proficient readers, like Beth's students, do this; basic readers usually don't.

Understanding information is the key to success in the twenty-first century. Not memorizing facts, but thinking critically about information. Doing the mental work with the author to create shared *and* individual understanding. Once your students know how to create understanding, they will be able to think about and understand the fact-filled texts they will encounter throughout their school years. They will think more critically, read more deeply, and handle assessments more effectively.

This chapter explores three issues that impact understanding: *the role of cognition, the role of language,* and *the role of the text.* It lays the conceptual groundwork for teaching the cognitive strategies in the remaining chapters—enabling you to move theory into practice.

The Role of Cognition

Have you ever wondered why it is that your students can read the same chapter in a science or social studies book, yet some can't remember any of the information, some can recite definitions but can't talk about the concepts, and still others can discuss in great depth almost everything they read? The extent to which a student retains, understands, and can discuss information in a text depends largely on how that information was processed (Caine & Caine, 1991; Kerry, 2002; Loftus & Loftus, 1976; Pressley & Woloshyn, 1995; Vockell, 1995). As teachers, we will be in a better position to help our students create understanding if we understand how cognition impacts learning.

As we read information, the brain determines whether to pay attention to the information or filter it out. If we decide to pay attention, the information enters working memory. Working memory, however, is limited in terms of the amount of information it can hold and the length of time it can hold that information. The brain must do something with the information to hold onto it or it will lose it. There are two things that it can do with the information: (a) continuously rehearse the information, or (b) shift the information into long-term memory (Kintsch, 1987; Kintsch, 1998; Loftus & Loftus, 1976; Pressley & Woloshyn, 1995; Vockell, 1995). What we cognitively choose to do with the information determines if we create understanding or not.

Continuously Rehearsing the Information: Teflon Learning

Rehearsing the information is what we do when we study information in order to memorize it. We go over and over it in our brain so that we can recall it. The information might be learned, but it is usually remembered temporarily since it is has not been stored in long-term memory.

With this type of learning, the brain is like Teflon because information just seems to slide right off it. This explains why, six weeks after the science test, our students can't remember the labels and definitions that they knew so well on the test. My students often could not recall how to spell a word in their writing that they had just correctly spelled the week before on a spelling test. And how many times did my students tell their teacher the following year, "She never taught us *that*!"? Teflon learning.

When students are rehearsing the information, there is no interaction between text and reader. No mental work done with the author. Rehearsing the information does not result in understanding.

Shifting the Information to Long-Term Memory: Velcro Learning

Truly understanding is all about making connections—connecting the new information to what has already been stored in long-term memory (Caine & Caine, 1991; Kintsch, 1987, 1994, 1998; Kintsch & van Dijk, 1978; Strickland & Morrow, 1989; Vockell, 1995). Connections are like Velcro for the new information. By moving the new information from short-term memory to long-term memory, we make the new information "stick."

We call information in long-term memory *prior knowledge*: memories of our past experiences, our beliefs and feelings, things we have learned over the years (Kintsch, 1994, 1998; Kintsch & van Dijk, 1978; Pearson & Fielding, 1991; Pearson, Roehler, Dole, & Duffy, 1992; Tierney & Pearson, 1994). I use a backpack to represent children's prior knowledge. Most children come to school these days carrying a backpack. Sometimes those backpacks are filled with everything they own (or so it seems!), and sometimes they contain little. In my eyes, children come to school with "cognitive backpacks" also, which are filled with bits and pieces of prior knowledge. And what is in those backpacks will impact their understanding of what they read.

Proficient readers create understanding by constantly connecting new information to the contents of their cognitive backpacks, so that the new information fits into whatever concept they are reading about. Velcro learning. For example, Joshua, the information-literate first grader described in Chapter 1, did more than memorize facts about spiders. He developed understanding about spiders through reading because he had spider-related prior knowledge in his backpack. He was able to connect the text to his earlier experiences of seeing spiders outside. He was able to comprehend the text more fully—and enjoy it—because he was already familiar with how spiders moved and what made one type of spider different from another.

Understanding, then, is ultimately about how students relate to a particular topic or idea. The extent of their understanding is determined by the extent of their connections (Henjy, 2004). Conversely, the more removed from prior knowledge the new information, the more likely students will simply memorize that information. The National Research Council's book *How People Learn* (Bransford, Brown, & Cocking, 2000) reports that if prior knowledge is not actively engaged, the learner might retain new information only short term or fail to grasp it at all. Understanding is all about making connections as the reader interacts with the text.

Using Thinking Skills to Make Connections

The cognitive strategies described in the rest of the book—predicting, observing, interpreting, connecting, and organizing—are "thinking skills" proficient readers use to make the connections necessary for creating understanding and, in the process, access, evaluate, and use information. Research confirms that these are strategies effective readers use (Kintsch, 1994, 1998; Kintsch & van Dijk, 1978; Pearson & Fielding, 1991; Pearson et al., 1992; Pressley & Woloshyn, 1995; Tierney & Pearson, 1994). In this book, you will learn how to scaffold learning in order to help students look for effective connections and apply them before, during, and after reading nonfiction.

The Role of Language

❝ I think once we discover the power of language, how children need to talk and share their thinking, and how important it is to their learning, we wonder how learning could have ever taken place in a quiet classroom. I mean, just giving them the book, copying it, and going on. It's hard to think about going back to that! You certainly can't use the word *quiet* about my class anymore!" Beth was reflecting on her teaching in her first-grade classroom. Beth's students had successfully learned how to interact with the text and with one another as they created understanding through the role of language.

Like cognition, language influences understanding greatly. By language, I mean oral language (speaking), receptive language (listening), and internal language (thinking).

In much of the last century, a quiet classroom was considered a good classroom. Students spoke mainly to answer questions. And those questions came quite infrequently—the average student answered a question only once every 10 hours of instruction (Graesser & Person, 1994). Language was used primarily as a means of assessing what we suspected students had learned. They answered questions after reading a chapter for science. They wrote paragraphs explaining what they learned in social studies. There was little verbal interaction. However, we know now that language helps us to learn. Language and thinking have a reciprocal effect (Vygotsky, 1986). In his book *To Think,* Frank Smith (1990) contends that you simply cannot separate the two: "Thought is always a part of language . . . language cannot be separated from thought."

Internal Language

As we read, write, and think, we are actually talking to ourselves. So the more language we have, the more it helps us to think. As proficient readers, we "talk to ourselves" as we try to make sense of the text. We have a silent, inner conversation with the text's author (Rosenblatt, 1994). We use internal language to find and make the connections from the new information we are reading to the known information stored in long-term memory. This inner conversation enables us to move information from our short-term memory into long-term memory (Keys, 1999; Osborne & Wittrock, 1983). Readers who engage in this kind of cognitive dialogue learn more effectively than those who do not (Vockell, 1995). Or, as Margaret Mooney (2003) contends, "Learning should come from a two-way dialogue and not from the author shouting in the reader's ear" (p. 48).

How, though, do young children learn to "talk to themselves"? How do they learn to use internal language to find relationships between what they know and what they are learning from reading? The process begins by first learning to talk with others. Cognitive interaction begins with social interaction. Talking is a key to learning how to understand (Vygotsky, 1986).

Expressive and Receptive Language

Receptive language is the language students receive, or hear, whereas expressive language, or talk, is the language they express. Research suggests that oral language helps to create new understanding (Keys, 1999; Strickland & Morrow, 1989).

Take into account how young children learn before they ever come to school. They learn best by talking about what they are doing. They make sense of the world as they explore it and talk about what they discover (Galda, Cullinan, & Strickland, 1993; Strickland & Morrow, 1989). Consider any 2-year-old child's favorite question, "Why?" which they ask in order to figure out what's going on around them.

My granddaughter Emily just turned 2. It is amazing to watch her. She has learned that her desires and experiences can be represented with language (and it's so much easier to communicate them with language). She has learned that objects, actions, and experiences have labels, such as *tree* (object), *run* (action), and *birthday party* (experience). And like all young children, as she develops she learns to use these labels, which are symbols, to represent the concrete.

When we give children opportunities to develop expressive and receptive language, we give them a way to engage in and represent thinking. Arthur Costa (1991) asserts that children with few opportunities for language development have more limited cognitive development than children who have many opportunities. Therefore, children's language impacts how they create understanding.

Psycholinguistic experts define language as consisting of two levels: *deep structure* (where meaning resides in the mind—the thought) and *surface structure* (the symbolic representation of the meaning that we see and hear—the language) (Chomsky, 1972). The brain has a much more difficult time processing information when that information remains at the surface-structure level and doesn't attach itself at the deep-structure level.

If students are learning information at the surface-structure level only, the result is word calling or rote memorization. At a surface-structure level, information does not attach to meaning at the deep-structure level, and the information will be stored in short-term memory with limited learning. While observing a third-grade class during science, I noticed the students were writing definitions for vocabulary words. Many copied the definition for the word *canyon*: "a deep gorge or precipice." Something told me they didn't have any deep structure attached to that word! Understanding requires connections to deep structures.

Language as Conversation

Creating understanding from text on our own is difficult; talking through the text with others facilitates understanding and helps students learn how to find connections for learning (Palinscar & Brown, 1984). Notice how conversation in Beth's class helped students get ready to read *Chickens Aren't the Only Ones* (Heller, 1999).

BETH: I notice that the title of our text is *Chickens Aren't the Only Ones*. That title makes me think of what other kinds of animals might go with chickens. Because if chickens aren't the only ones, then I think the author will tell us about other animals that are somehow connected to chickens.

JOSEPH: Maybe a Chinese water dragon might be in there.

BETH: What makes you say that, Joséph? Why do you think the author would include them in this book?

JOSEPH: It lays eggs like a chicken.

CHLOE: I don't think it will go that far into reptiles. I think it will just include things that are in the bird family. I don't think it will go that far.

JOSEPH: They might go that far.

BETH: What makes you say it will go that far?

JOSEPH: Because the title says that chickens aren't the only ones.

BETH: So you are thinking that it could include other animals. What would they have in common?

MATT: As long as they laid eggs they could be in there.

SASHA: It could be about pigs, too.

BETH: What makes you say pigs, Sasha?

SASHA: Because they go with chickens.

BETH: Tell us how they go with chickens.

SASHA: They all live on the farm, and if chickens aren't the only ones, maybe they are talking about the farm.

BETH: That would make sense.

MATT: But pigs don't lay eggs and cows don't lay eggs and lambs don't.

BETH: So these animals don't have anything to do with laying eggs, but how do these animal go together with chickens?

SEAN:	They all live on a farm.
SASHA:	See, they go together.
BETH:	And right now we aren't sure about the information because we are predicting. So does it make sense that we might read about pigs because they go with chickens?
MATT:	And what about owls? They can live on a farm AND lay eggs.

In the classroom, talk is developed as conversation. This involves listening to others and responding to what was said as students talk through the text.

These types of classroom conversations are critical for our young students. Children are coming to school with fewer social interactions at home, and consequently fewer experiences with conversation (Hallowell, 2006; Tapscott, 1999; Wallis, 2006) and less language available for creating understanding.

Conversations are initially guided by the teacher as interactions between students and teacher. This soon shifts to interactions among students, as children learn to talk through the text with one another. The ultimate goal is for children to internalize the talk and learn to have inner conversations as they interact with the text and the author.

Language as Metacognitive Dialogue

Talking through the text leads to understanding and talking through our thinking leads to metacognition. If you provide students with opportunities for such talk, they should internalize that talk, and be using it on a regular basis to create understanding by the time they reach the upper-elementary grades. They

The Benefits of Conversation

→ Provides a starting point for learning how to understand

→ Helps students make connections that they may not have made on their own and consequently expand their understanding

→ Helps students discover language (surface structure) to describe their connections (deep structure)

→ Helps students know if they know (if they cannot tell in their own words what they read, then they probably did not understand it)

will also be more likely to meet those fourth-grade expectations on state and national assessments that ask them to not only give the answer but to write a paragraph explaining how the answer was obtained. They will struggle with this unless they have first learned to talk with others about their thinking.

Costa says, "Realizing that thinking is basic and that children's early language (and therefore cognitive) development may be lacking, we are witnessing a new direction for classroom instruction: increasing verbal interaction" (1991). Cognitive strategy instruction embraces the important role of language that Costa points out. It also capitalizes on the way young children talk about the environment around them in order to learn about the world.

The cognitive strategies described in the remaining chapters are designed to help you create the kinds of conversations that move students toward understanding. Indeed, talk is an integral part of cognitive strategy instruction. It helps students glean meaning from the information they are reading.

The Role of the Text

"If this is nonfiction, then why did the author put a sun with a smile and some eyes and a nose on the front?" This wise question was raised by Angelica during a conversation in Beth's classroom about how nonfiction looks different than stories. The conversation continued this way:

Chris:	It could be fiction.
Lizzie:	Maybe she just wanted to decorate.
Anna:	Like that book of stars. The author put a picture of a bear.
Margo:	But I think that it's nonfiction because *The Planets* sounds like nonfiction. And it has pictures of the planets and the Milky Way, and so it's nonfiction.
Beth:	So do you think it was a good idea for the author to put a smiley face? Would you do that?
Angelica:	No, it's not real enough. It's not a photograph.
Lizzie:	Because she did that to be cute.
Sean:	Maybe they didn't have a real picture of a sun.
Anna:	I think it's nonfiction because it's about facts.
Angelica:	But she shouldn't have put that smiley face on the front.

MARGO:	The author tells facts about the planets.
ISAAC:	And see, there's a table of contents.
JOSHUA:	It's also nonfiction because scientists did the studying about planets.

Beth knows that the role of the text impacts her students' understanding of information. As children develop cognition and language for creating understanding, they also need to develop text knowledge—how text works.

One of the major obstacles primary students face when they encounter nonfiction is, plain and simple, knowing how to read the text. Sure, they may be able to say the words, but often they are unable to create understanding of the information from the text. The RAND report (*Reading for Understanding*, 2002) suggests why this is so: "When too many text factors are not matched to the reader's knowledge and experience, the text may be too difficult to comprehend." And students may not have that knowledge and experience because the books they're typically assigned are not informational. In other words, they have had little experience with nonfiction, so they have little or no knowledge about how it works (Dreher, 2003; Duke & Kays, 1998; Newkirk, 1989).

What kind of text knowledge do young readers need to create understanding with nonfiction? First, it is important that young readers know the ways nonfiction text works differently from fiction. Nonfiction and fiction texts look different, contain different features, and are organized differently. They require different comprehension skills and therefore the reader must apply cognitive strategies differently. You cannot learn how to read and write biography and then expect to be able to read and write poetry any more than you can learn to read and write fiction and expect to read and write nonfiction. To learn how to read nonfiction requires explicit instruction and multiple opportunities in the specific nonfiction genres (Duke, 2000). We must make clear the differences in how stories and nonfiction work.

Genre

"I can't make sense of this story!" Neale shouted as he threw his book down on his bed. "I don't get the characters. I can't figure out what's going on!" His mother recounted the incident to me. It seemed that Neale had checked out a nonfiction book on spiders and was trying to read it as he would a story. He subconsciously tried to take his text knowledge of stories and apply it to information. His lack of experience with text type impeded his understanding.

Teaching the Information Generation

As primary teachers, we may not even realize how much we are immersed in story and, consequently, how much our young students are immersed in it. Consider the following:

Children need explicit instruction about how nonfiction works.

- ◆ The majority of elementary teachers use narrative text for literacy instruction.

- ◆ Out of 500 classrooms nationwide, none of the most frequently read titles for read-alouds were nonfiction.

- ◆ In a study of first-grade classrooms, less than 3 percent of what was visible on the classroom walls was nonfiction.

- ◆ Classroom libraries have only approximately 10 percent nonfiction books available to students.

- ◆ New basals contain only 12 percent nonfiction texts.

- ◆ Eighty percent of teachers surveyed reported they did not use nonfiction in their elementary classroom because it was "too hard."

  (Dreher, 2003; Duke, 2000; Hoffman et al., 1994; Hoffman, Roser, & Battle, 1993; Kamil & Lane, 1997)

A look around most elementary classrooms will likely confirm these research findings. Why are stories so popular? It could be that we're comfortable with them. Many of us assume that when students learn how to read with fiction, they easily transfer those reading skills to nonfiction.

In fact, our teacher language reflects this assumption. I have noticed that most elementary teachers call all texts "stories"—and I was guilty of this in the classroom as well! During science, I would tell my students that we were reading a story about volcanoes or a story about space. In reality, the texts were informational. Jane Rothery (1996) documented this phenomenon in her study. She found that teachers mostly identified texts as "stories," but did use the term "reports" for students' writing of information. However, she also found that teachers had a difficult time identifying the criteria for a story or for a report. She found that teachers could not articulate the text knowledge for each genre.

Although most of our instruction is with story, most of our state and national reading assessments, 70 to 80 percent of them, in fact, are based on nonfiction (Daniels & Zemelman, 2004). And the emphasis on nonfiction doesn't stop there. According to Galda et al. (1993), "Students read more nonfiction books in science, social studies, and math than they do in all categories of fiction combined. School and public libraries contain 85 percent nonfiction and only 15 percent fiction. Statewide assessments of reading test students almost entirely on nonfiction selections. During a lifetime, we probably read twice as much nonfiction as fiction" (p. 211).

Despite this fact, by third grade, children have had four to five years of immersion in story. Is it any wonder that Neale was expecting characters and story structure when he opened his nonfiction book? It is important that we make the distinctions about nonfiction text clear to our young students. Nonfiction looks different, contains different features, and is organized differently, and therefore must be read differently. The following sections will outline some specific textual differences that impact understanding: organization, features, and layout.

Organization

When we pick up a story, we begin at the beginning and read straight through. It is important to do this because, at the beginning, the author introduces the characters, setting, and problem. However, we usually don't read nonfiction that way. Instead, we often read only parts. Rather than reading from beginning to end, we interact with the information in a variety of ways, depending on the purpose for reading. For example, to prepare for a safari in Kenya, I might read a book about animals from around the world, searching between the table of contents, the text, the index, pictures, captions, diagrams, and headings to find only the information on African mammals. This up-and-down, back-and-forth reading requires different reading strategies than the straight-through kind of reading of fiction. It also requires the reader to do the mental work of connecting the text and the features.

As with Neale, students often have difficulty accessing information because of their prior knowledge and expectations about story. Once students have internalized a basic understanding of story structure, they can anticipate the organization of most fiction genres: historical fiction, science fiction, realistic fiction, mysteries, folktales, and fantasies. On the other hand, nonfiction can be structured in many different ways: descriptive, cause and effect, sequential, problem and solution, alphabetical—just to name a few. And most of those structures can be applied to the different genres of nonfiction, including instructions, explanations, persuasive texts, essays, fact books, reference books, magazines, biography, information books, news articles, journals, and diaries. It can seem confusing and overwhelming to young readers (and older ones alike!).

Proficient readers think about the text as well the information that they are reading in the text. In today's classroom, readers are expected to do the following:

- Determine why and how the text was developed

- Understand how it is organized as a way to make sense of the text

- Comprehend the entire text as well as pieces of it, and understand how those pieces relate

(Reading Framework for the 2003 National Assessment of Educational Progress, 2003)

Our young readers need cognitive tools to know how to think about the text while they think about the content.

Features

Because there is usually so much information in nonfiction texts, authors and editors include access features such as headings, charts, tables, maps, photographs, diagrams, captions, and indexes to help the reader develop understanding of the text.

Specifically, access features help us to find the information that we need efficiently and effectively. Like maps, they help us find our way through the vast amount of information in the text. They help us determine where we are going by shining a spotlight on individual bits of information, showing us how those bits are connected, and summarizing those bits into one sensible whole. They help us to compare information, to visualize information, and to organize information in our minds. As proficient readers we use these features to access and evaluate the information.

I've found that children often know the definitions for access features, but may not be familiar with how to use them. In fact, basic readers often overlook and ignore them. They do not have the cognitive tools for knowing how to access and evaluate information using these features. This is why it is important to teach in ways that go beyond simply defining access features.

Layout

Take a look at nonfiction trade books and textbooks published prior to 1995, and then compare them to more recent books. You will immediately notice a difference in the layout—or the interior design. You might notice that the newer books are more engaging and inviting for young readers because of the amount of color, the number of graphics, and the size and style of the type that the designer chose to use. These changes are intentional on the part of the book companies because today's students expect text to support graphics, not graphics to support text (Prensky, 2001b). Therefore, layouts are much more visual than they used to be.

Furthermore, there have been more subtle changes in the layout of these books as well. In her study of nonfiction texts, Sharon Walpole (1998) found that graphics in books published prior to 1995 reiterated the information in the running text, which meant that the connections between the graphics and running text were usually obvious. However, today's texts put responsibility on the reader for making connections. They require inferencing to integrate the ideas in the text and the information in the text, visuals, and headings.

What this means is that access features used to be optional. They were made available in case the reader wanted to confirm his or her understanding of the text. However, in today's books, important information is often found only in the access features—information that is needed for developing a full understanding of the text.

This means that readers must know how to use these features to create understanding. Readers must know to read between the access features and the running text to make

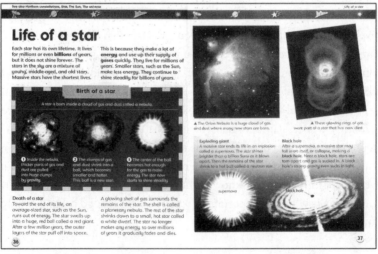

This is an example of a nonfiction text layout that is more graphic than layouts of the past.

critical inferences. They must understand the purpose of the features, the kind of information contained in them, and how the pieces of information relate, so they can understand the text in its entirety.

When we teach cognitive strategies in combination with text knowledge, we move students past first base in their thinking. Students learn that features not only give them access to the new information, but help them to connect and evaluate the information, and make inferences based on it. They learn to interpret new information in light of their prior knowledge. They learn how to do the mental work with the text and the author to create individual and shared understanding.

Closing Thoughts

Have you seen the cartoon of the little boy with a book in his hand, asking his teacher, "You mean we have to read it *and* comprehend it?" In today's world, our students must do exactly that. Specifically, they must interact with the text, connect new information to prior knowledge, analyze text features, recognize how information is organized, and have a metacognitive conversation with the author in order to comprehend! A big goal, for sure. It is more critical than ever to understand the role of cognition, language, and text in creating understanding to help students reach that goal.

The cognitive strategies introduced in the following chapters will help our Information Generation students move toward proficiency. Students will learn how nonfiction text works. They will learn how to evaluate nonfiction literally, critically, and conceptually. They will be able to access information efficiently and effectively and to evaluate information critically and competently. They will become information literate.

Today's nonfiction text:

→ Contains more complex connections among ideas, requiring more inferencing on the reader's part

→ Puts more responsibility on the reader to integrate ideas

→ Contains features that have shifted from labeling to elaborating ideas

→ Has shifted from providing explicit information to implicit relationships

→ Offers access features that contain new information

(Walpole, 1998)

CHAPTER 3

Teaching for Understanding:
An Overview of Cognitive Strategy Instruction

I t is spring at Mandeville Elementary, a K–3 school. A walk past several classrooms offers a glimpse into information literacy in action. Brandi Appe is on the floor, leading her kindergartners in a sorting activity of bear facts from the text that they read. Michelle McHale reads aloud a book about communities to her third graders. As the students analyze how the author organized the information, she charts their responses. Sharon Becnel's first graders are paired around the room reading to one another about ladybugs. The room is abuzz with activity as partners finish reading and then sort the information they gathered. Debbie Sterling moves from group to group in her second-grade classroom, observing small groups talking about penguins and recording their thoughts in learning logs. Next door, Judy Hankel's second graders are spread around the room discussing which type of organizer to use for their penguin project, while Judy offers suggestions. Beth confers with one of her first-grade students, Matt, during writer's workshop about his piece on sharks. She asks him to explain why he decided to use a sequential organizer for his writing.

Information literacy is in full swing. These primary students are learning to access information efficiently and effectively, to evaluate it critically and competently, and to use information creatively and accurately (*Information Literacy Standards for Student Learning*, 1998). These teachers are modeling strategies for their students, creating conversations that will eventually lead to internal language, and making explicit how nonfiction works. They are teaching for understanding with cognitive strategy instruction.

Research confirms that readers make significant gains in comprehension when they are given cognitive strategy instruction (Pressley, Johnson, Symons, McGoldrick, & Kurita, 1989; Pressley & Woloshyn, 1995; Rosenhine, Meier, & Chapman, 1996; Rosenhine & Meister, 1994). The National Reading Panel (*Report of the National Reading Panel*, 2000) states that, to be effective, this instruction should do the following:

- Cover specific strategies

- Include explicit instruction in those strategies
- Be systematic until students can carry out those strategies independently

The remaining chapters provide you with teaching tools, texts, and contexts to do all of the above in order to create information-literate students. The chapter titles are intended to reflect the information literacy standards (as discussed in Chapter 1) and the cognitive strategy being developed:

Chapter 4: Predicting to Access Information

Chapter 5: Evaluating Text for Literal Understanding

Chapter 6: Evaluating Text for Critical Understanding

Chapter 7: Evaluating Text for Conceptual Understanding

Specifically, each chapter does the following:

- Introduces the strategy and shows how it helps students access, evaluate, and use information

- Offers ways to teach the strategy explicitly by breaking it down into manageable steps and providing ideas for introducing, applying, and assessing it

- Provides teaching tools and routines to make instruction systematic to move students toward independence with strategy use

This chapter could be considered the manual for strategy instruction. It gives an overview of the teaching tools (*What will I use to teach the strategies?*), the texts (*What kinds of nonfiction should I use for teaching strategies?*), and the contexts I use in Chapters 4 through 7 (*When in my schedule and classroom will I teach strategy instruction?*). This overview will help you to determine how to utilize the rest of the book to best meet your teaching needs.

Teaching Tools for Information Literacy

As teachers, we need tools to teach cognitive strategies to this Information Generation. Tools for:

- Making thinking visible
- Organizing and recording thinking
- Developing, guiding, and focusing talk

These tools are used across strategies. I will describe them in more detail in the following chapters, as they relate to specific strategies.

Tools for Making Thinking Visible

Good teachers know how to take a complex process and break it down for a novice—whether dancing the tango, shooting baskets, playing piano, or learning a strategy. Learning a strategy, however, differs from most other types of activities in that what we are teaching is an invisible process. A dance instructor shows his students how to keep the knees bent as he dances the tango with his partner. A basketball coach shows her players how to plant their feet and extend their elbows to release a free throw. A piano teacher demonstrates the complex fingering for a difficult portion of a recital piece. And we as teachers must also break the process down into manageable steps and make each step explicit for creating understanding—for thinking. We must make the invisible visible. These tools—think-alouds, modeling, and explanations—can help us do that.

Think-Alouds

To introduce a cognitive strategy and make it explicit, the teacher thinks out loud his *own* thinking process, putting each step in language young readers can understand. A think-aloud involves talking about the cognitive strategy you are using within the context of the text you are reading (Wilhelm, 2001). It is to show students how good readers think while reading.

VICKI: When I looked at the cover of this book, the first thing I read is the title, *Manatees and Dugongs*. I immediately thought, "What in the world is a dugong?" You see, I noticed the photo of a manatee on the front cover, and I knew it was a manatee because I saw manatees when I visited Florida. But now I am wondering: What does a dugong have to do with a manatee? So I open the table of contents hoping to find some more information.

Think-Aloud Teacher Language

Since the purpose of this phase is to make the teacher's thinking process explicit, use "I" when speaking to children:

➜ "I'm thinking that . . ."

➜ "First, I look for . . ."

➜ "Before I begin reading, I . . ."

➜ "I noticed in the photo . . ."

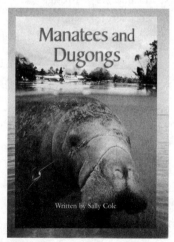

Vicki used *Manatees and Dugongs* (Cole, 2000) for her think-aloud.

With information-literacy instruction, a think-aloud also involves thinking out loud about how the nonfiction text works as you think about the content and the strategy. The teacher is thinking aloud about how he multitasks with text, moving between the content, his thinking, and knowing how the text works. Specific examples for thinking aloud each strategy are provided in the appropriate chapter.

Modeling

As the teacher thinks aloud his own process of thinking using the strategy being emphasized, the teacher models how to use the strategy. Modeling requires breaking the strategy down into manageable steps and showing young readers just how the strategy works. Each chapter will show specific ways to break down the strategies to introduce them to students.

Explanations

Just as the basketball coach explains how stance impacts a free throw, explanations should accompany the think-aloud as the teacher explains how reading works (Duffy, 1993). This helps students to link "this is what I am doing" to "this is what you should do."

VICKI: Let's talk about why we are doing what we are going to do. You are learning how to be good readers, and good readers think about the information before they begin reading. They look at the heading first and think about what they already know about the topic.

The Value of Explanations

Explaining how good readers think about their thinking in order to understand the information is enormously helpful to students.

→ "As we read about volcanoes today, we will look for clues to predict. Good readers look for clues before they read, in order to think about the information."

→ "Good readers read information slowly and thoughtfully in order to think about the information. As we read about the different kinds of rock, we will read a bit and then stop and think."

→ "I like how you shifted your thinking as you read more about planets and space. Good readers change their thinking as they get new information."

The teacher also should share why this strategy helps her as a reader. She constantly relates the strategy to what good readers do. She helps students to see that a good reader understands the content better because of using the thinking strategy. The teacher's role is to create understanding of the task and to help students figure out why this strategy works.

Tools for Organizing and Recording Thinking

In addition to think-alouds, modeling, and explanations, we need to use teaching tools that capture student thinking in writing—tools such as anchor charts, GO! Charts, sticky notes, and learning logs. These tools, which I introduce on the next pages and apply to specific strategies in the next chapters, help students to become aware of their thinking and make it visible, just as think-alouds and modeling make the teacher's thinking visible. They are critical in helping our Information Generation students learn to focus and organize their thinking, which is often bombarded by all this information—an issue that can impede their learning from text, as discussed in Chapter 1.

Anchor Charts

It is important for young readers to "see" their thinking, and so I have learned to anchor their thinking with charting. Anchor charts are tools for recording student thinking. They allow the teacher to hold students' thinking and provide physical tracks of student learning. As the teacher guides the conversation, he records students' responses. Charting slows down the thinking process, allowing both teacher and student to focus more on what is being said.

These charts provide anchor points to refer back to and from which teachers can craft student thinking and then further develop the content. This pushes students toward becoming more conscious of their own thinking and of the cognitive processes they are using as they create understanding. Charting also provides a model for how to record thinking, which students will eventually learn to do with sticky notes and learning logs.

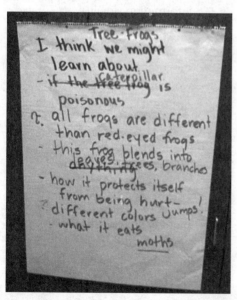

This anchor chart was used for recording thinking before and after reading.

Charting is used in each chapter for introducing and developing each strategy with students. Anchor charts are best used to focus and develop a specific strategy. Suggestions will be made in each chapter for ways to use anchor charts to record and develop student thinking for each strategy.

GO! Charts

GO! Charts are expanded anchor charts intended to visually organize the thinking process before, during, and after reading a text (Benson & Cummins, 2000). The term "GO! Chart" stands for *graphic organizer chart*. This has proven to be a powerful teaching tool for helping Information Generation students to develop, organize, and internalize cognitive strategies by visually organizing their thinking. It helps children become aware of what good readers do as they read, and makes them conscious of their own thinking process.

The GO! Chart is actually six anchor charts combined into one large graphic organizer. It is usually made from bulletin board paper or butcher paper that is divided into six columns approximately 90 inches wide. Each column represents one of the strategies for developing understanding: *Predictions, Vocabulary, Understanding, Interpretations, Connections,* and *Organizing.* The systematic use of the GO! Chart teaches children to internalize the format of the chart, which facilitates their cognitive development and focuses their attention as they read.

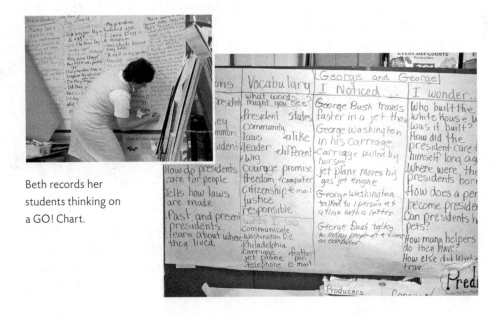

Beth records her students thinking on a GO! Chart.

Predictions	Vocabulary	Understanding	Interpretations	Connections	Organizing

The following strategy chapters are laid out to follow the GO! Chart organization. The strategies in each chapter can be used separately, with thinking recorded on anchor charts, or with the entire process recorded and reflected on the GO! Chart. Each chapter gives specific suggestions for how to incorporate the GO! Chart in strategy instruction.

When children have had multiple opportunities for the teacher to model recording thinking on the GO! Chart, then responsibility is shifted to students for organizing and recording their own thinking.

Sticky Notes

As responsibility for recording thinking is gradually released to children, sticky notes are used to have students "hold the pen" and "hold their thinking." This allows them to write in short, focused ways while the teacher still guides the conversation. Initially, students write their thinking on sticky notes and place them on the anchor chart or GO! Chart. Eventually, students record their thinking as they read the text in a learning log. Then they bring their thinking to the conversation in small groups or to the whole group.

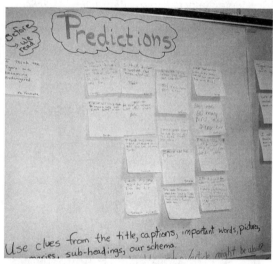

Students record predictions on sticky notes.

Learning Logs

As children write their thinking, learning logs provide places to record the information they are learning and to record their thinking about the information. Students are intended to record learning and thinking as it occurs, similar to how they often use sticky notes during reading. Learning logs can be designed as T-charts, or they can reflect the

Teaching the Information Generation

format of the GO! Chart so that students know how to focus and organize their thinking as they read. An example of a learning log is included in the appendix, on pages 214 and 215, and below.

Learning logs are intended as learning tools. However, they also provide feedback to the teacher about strategy instruction and content learning. Teachers can use them to determine what content the students learned, to identify students' misconceptions about the content, and to find out how the students are applying the strategy.

Children should work in pairs or small groups to develop their learning logs, as this creates a context for conversations about the information and the text. If children complete their learning logs independently while reading, they need to have opportunities to bring their learning logs and their thinking to a small-group discussion about the text. As discussed in the previous chapter, it is critical that children talk through the text in order to create their understanding of the new information.

Second graders record their thinking in learning logs as they read and talk about spiders.

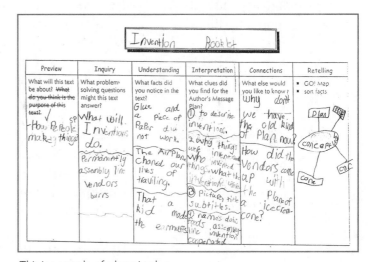

This is a sample of a learning log.

Tools for Developing, Guiding, and Focusing Talk

Most children are not accustomed to talking through text. Rather, they typically expect the teacher to ask questions during or after a reading and their classmates to give correct answers. However, with cognitive strategy instruction, the teacher provides opportunities to develop, guide, and focus thoughtful talk about text. The teacher encourages large-group, small-group, and paired conversations that will lead to the all-important inner conversations that I discussed earlier.

Using "You"-Focused Language

Teacher language is more "you" focused at this point and should direct students' attention to what is important in the text and what they need to focus on as they read and apply the strategy.

➤ "I think you said . . ."

➤ "It sounds like you . . ."

➤ "Is this what you mean?"

➤ "What makes you say that?"

➤ "How did you know that?"

➤ "Can you help me find . . .?"

➤ "I think . . . What do you think?"

Group Conversations

The teacher invites students to participate with the thinking and discussion to create conversations about the content using the strategy being developed. Michael Pressley (2002) reminds us that "strategies are vehicles for coordinating dialogue about text."

Teacher language shifts from a monologue with the think-aloud to more of a dialogue with the students. Conversations are created when the teacher initiates questions that invite students to participate in thinking about both the content and the text. The teacher follows up student responses to encourage elaboration and conversation.

Students need to hear their thinking, so it is important to repeat and rephrase what students say as they respond. This also allows the teacher to craft both the language and thinking of the children. Isabel Beck and Margaret McKeown (2001) found that this also extends children's talk and invites others to participate.

Quicktalk Pair and Share

At different points during instruction, students turn to their neighbor and conduct a "Quicktalk." Students are given a short amount of time (one to two minutes), and the rule is that they must talk about the topic given until the teacher calls time. This allows students to talk in a focused and frequent way, allowing them to access connections and to practice putting their thinking into language. Also, students who might not normally respond in a large group are usually willing to talk with their neighbor. Short time periods of about 60 seconds really push kids to get right to the task (and work wonders with boys and their competitive nature). "The clock's ticking, so start talking" is like the starting gun for the beginning of a race!

Partners and Sticky Notes

Students often feel comfortable talking with partners before they are ready to talk within a larger group. When you pair partners and sticky notes, children begin to assume more

This student is recording a collaborative prediction.

responsibility for the thinking, talking, and writing. This is a powerful bridge to having students write their thinking in learning logs independently.

Students talk through their thinking with one another first and then record their thinking on a sticky note. For example, Levi and Kenya were discussing their predictions about a magazine article on Pluto. They talked through their thinking in order to consider possibilities.

KENYA:	I think it's about Pluto.
LEVI:	Duh! Of course it's about Pluto. It says right there. But we have to figure out what it might *be* about Pluto.
KENYA:	I think they will send a spaceship to Pluto.
LEVI:	And what will we say about why we think that?
KENYA:	It has a picture of a rocket. Maybe they will explore Pluto with this rocket.
LEVI:	So what will we write down?
KENYA:	Let's say that "rockets will go to Pluto."
LEVI:	But you know Ms. C will ask us WHY.
KENYA:	Okay. Then say that "rockets will go to Pluto to explore."

The boys decided on a prediction to record on their sticky note that they would share with the rest of the class. They knew from much modeling that they needed to be able to tell the rest of the group how they came up with that prediction. When students work together to record a collaborative response, it allows them to build on each other's ideas, thinking, and language. It also pushes students to work toward consensus, an important component of collaborative small groups.

Quickwrites

Quickwrites can be used to jumpstart conversations by accessing prior knowledge and getting language going. As with Quicktalks, a short amount of time is given to focus thinking, usually one or two minutes. The teacher asks a specific question for students to consider. For example, before reading the article mentioned above, the teacher might ask one of these questions for the Quickwrite:

- Have you ever thought about going to space? What would it be like to travel in space?

- What do you know about Pluto or other planets in our solar system?

- How do you think scientists might explore a planet that is far away?

Then, when time starts, students must write their thinking for the entire one or two minutes. Children are told not to stop writing until the end of the one- or two-minute time frame. The idea is to get them to write continuously for the allotted time. The more children do Quickwrites, the more they are using their internalized language.

Quickwrites can also be used to record learning after reading. However, here they are used as a tool to facilitate conversation.

Texts and Contexts for Teaching Information Literacy

Texts and contexts are the *what, where,* and *when* of cognitive strategy instruction. They help us answer questions such as *What texts should I use? Where is the best place to introduce strategies? And once I do, when is the best time for students to begin applying them?* This section is designed to answer these types of questions.

Texts for Teaching Information Literacy

When introducing and having students apply cognitive strategies, I've found that *informational text* is the best type of nonfiction text to use. The primary purpose of informational text is to share information about the natural or social world by describing attributes of a topic (such as fish, spiders, or animals of Africa) or processes or events connected to a topic (such as electricity, simple machines, or the digestive system) (Pappas, 2006). Informational text usually has common linguistic and text features

(Duke & Bennett-Armistead, 2003; Pappas, 2006), such as a table of contents, an index, headings, and visuals, which I will explore in the following chapters. It also requires the types of reading strategies demanded of nonfiction text, as discussed in Chapter 2, such as reading back and forth between the text and the visuals and reading the information in pieces.

Most young children gravitate toward informational text as they learn about the world around them. It seems that the dinosaur books and space books are the first ones to go out of the library on library day. Take advantage of their interests in informational text and teach children how to create understanding by connecting the text to concepts that might already be in their cognitive backpacks.

Once students apply strategies to access, evaluate, and use information from informational text, they can do so with other types of nonfiction, such as biography, instructions, and persuasive text. The teaching tools described throughout the book work well with most all types of nonfiction text.

The Context for Introducing Strategies: Shared Read-Aloud

In her book *Reading Essentials*, Regie Routman (2003) recommends shared read-aloud for most strategy teaching and demonstrations, describing it as "a purposeful teaching, discussing activity," and I agree. Shared read-aloud is a powerful context for introducing cognitive strategies, engaging in conversations, and making explicit how informational text works. It combines reading aloud with guided discussions to develop thinking. The teacher reads the text aloud and models, thinks aloud, and explains the cognitive strategy—usually

Choosing a Text for Shared Read-Aloud

➜ Topic should relate to content area, state benchmarks, or interests of children.

➜ Text can be above instructional level of children, as long as content is appropriate and engaging.

➜ Text should have engaging visuals and other important nonfiction text features.

➜ Books should be easily viewed for both text and visuals.

➜ Big Books, transparencies, or individual copies are good for shared read-alouds.

to the whole group, but it can also be carried out with small groups. It works equally well in any content area or in the literacy block.

Hearing the text, as opposed to reading it themselves, allows children to focus solely on what the text contains, how it's written, and how it works. As such, they can attend to their developing thinking and language (Routman, 2003). As children become more comfortable with the cognitive strategy being introduced, responsibility for reading the text is transferred to children through the context of guided practice.

The Context for Applying Strategies: Guided Practice

Guided practice allows students to try out the strategy that has been modeled and explained through several shared read-aloud sessions. Students hold more responsibility for reading and thinking. Guided practice can be done individually or with partners as the teacher roves the room providing support as needed, or it can be conducted with small groups that the teacher creates. The intent is to connect the whole-group strategy

Choosing a Text for Guided Practice

Choosing the text for guided practice is critical to children's success in gaining more control of the strategy.

→ The text should allow children to be able to focus their energies on the developing strategy without too much challenge from the written text. For guided practice, Routman suggests a text that is "not so long it is overwhelming for students or so complex that it requires substantial background explanation" (2003, p. 154).

→ If buddy reading, the text should have 95 percent known words (independent reading level).

→ If working with teacher support in small-group instruction, then 90 percent known words (instructional level) is usually sufficient.

→ Leveled texts or short articles from instructional magazines (such as *Time for Kids, Scholastic News,* or *National Geographic Explorer*) are good resources for trying out the strategy in the context of guided practice.

demonstrations to small-group strategy application, or to create circular teaching (Dorn & Soffos, 2005).

For cognitive strategy instruction to be effective we must provide practice opportunities with a variety of texts in different contexts across the curriculum and throughout the day. Students should apply individual strategies to Big Books, articles, trade books, and textbooks for various content areas. The more opportunities students have for this type of work, the more they come to realize that strategies are powerful learning tools. It's like one of our elementary students said: "Are you sure this is science? It sure feels a whole lot like reading!" Cognitive strategy instruction is teaching information with literacy and teaching literacy with information.

Using Teaching Tools, Texts, and Contexts to Provide Different Levels of Support

At the start of this chapter, I showed how teachers at Mandeville Elementary were teaching students how to organize information and, in the process, create understanding by using various informational texts, contexts, and teaching tools. Each teacher made conscious choices about the tools she used and how she used them, according to the level of support her students needed.

♦ Brandi and Michelle are *introducing the strategy* of organizing in the context of a shared read-aloud. They hold most of the responsibility for learning at this point. Brandi models and explains how to sort, while Michelle does the same for how to analyze an informational text for key concepts. Both teachers use a GO! Chart to help students become aware of their thinking.

♦ Sharon is helping students *apply the strategy to their own reading*. Her students have seen her model how to sort information and have done that activity as a whole group on several occasions. Now they are ready to try it out in pairs with information from their own reading—and with support, guidance, and feedback. Debbie is working with her students in small-group contexts, applying the strategy of organizing to their reading about penguins. They are using learning logs to record their thinking and to organize the information from the text about penguins.

♦ Judy is *applying the strategy of organizing to her students' writing*. They have been working with graphic organizers for weeks as she has modeled and constructed graphic organizers with the class during shared read-alouds. They are now ready to try them out more independently.

♦ Beth is *assessing the strategy* of organizing. Her first graders know "Don't pick up a pencil until you have a plan." Organizing is central in her writer's workshop. Her students have worked for months on the different ways to organize information and have also received a lot of modeling and many opportunities to try them out. Beth is now assessing Matt's ability to organize his writing. He tells her that he chose a sequential organizer because he wants to tell the order in which a shark finds and eats its food.

Each of these teachers had to decide how to use teaching tools, learning contexts, and informational texts with her students in conjunction with the level of support each student needed to grasp the strategy fully. In other words, they sought to match instruction to each student's needs.

Chapters 4 through 7 will help you match instruction to your own students' needs. These chapters will help you decide how you will teach the strategies within your curriculum, gradually moving students from full support provided by you to complete independence. With an eye toward reaching that goal, each chapter is organized around the following framework:

♦ Understanding the Strategy: An Overview

♦ Teaching the Strategy: A Way to Introduce and Develop the Strategy

♦ Trying Out the Strategy: Ideas for Helping Students Apply the Strategy to Reading and Writing

♦ Assessing the Strategy: Behaviors to Look for in Student Reading and Writing

Understanding the Strategy: An Overview

The first section of each chapter will describe the cognitive strategy, or strategies, to be introduced and briefly discuss its importance. It is critical for us as teachers to understand the why of the strategy so that we can not only explain to our students how we use the strategy, but also why it's important to use it. Pressley (Pressley & Woloshyn, 1995) maintains that "whether students come to value the strategies they are learning, and thus continue to use them after instruction ends, depends largely on the student recognizing their performance improves because they are using the strategies" (p. 247).

This section also includes a metaphor, or a "mind picture" as I call it, that I have found successful in introducing the strategy. A mind picture helps students connect a concrete example of something in their world to something new that they are learning. I earlier used the metaphors of Teflon and Velcro to explain how the brain works with learning. Jeffrey Wilhelm (2002) contends that "all learning is a metaphor: We must connect the already known to something new to achieve it" (p. 45). In each chapter I will provide a metaphor, or mind picture, and explain how you can use it to introduce and develop the strategy.

Teaching the Strategy: A Way to Introduce and Develop the Strategy

This section of each chapter shows you how to teach the cognitive strategy. It is about making students aware of the strategy—even overly aware at this early point. Suggestions are given for explaining and modeling the strategy within the learning context of the shared read-aloud. This section will break down the strategy into manageable steps to show your young readers just how the strategy works.

During this phase, the teacher holds both the book and the pen. She reads the text, guides the thinking, and helps create understanding of the information. She invites her students to listen to her think-alouds and explanations and to participate in the conversation. She records children's thinking on the anchor chart or GO! Chart as she guides, directs, and redirects her students.

Students need repeated experiences with the strategy, especially at the beginning stages. Several sessions modeling the same strategy and thinking out loud with a new text are required. Students will also need re-explanations, as they often will not get it on the first go-round or will possibly misunderstand part of the strategy (Duffy, 1993, 2002; Pressley, 2002).

Trying Out the Strategy: Ideas for Helping Students Apply the Strategy to Reading and Writing

In order for children to develop complex thinking skills, they need someone to show them how to use what they know in their own reading and writing. It is important to balance explicit instruction with lots of time for application (Routman, 2003). In fact, this is where the majority of time should be allotted for strategy instruction. Teachers tend to want to go directly from introducing a strategy to independent application of the strategy.

This part of each chapter provides suggestions for applying the strategy to students' own reading and writing. Some of the ideas are intended to further develop the thinking and language necessary for the students to apply the strategy. Others are intended to support students who need further guidance (basic and below-basic readers), while still others are intended to challenge more proficient readers or extend the learning.

This part of strategy instruction is intended to move students into the learning context of guided practice. The learner begins to take hold of the book to try out the developing strategy. Responsibility for learning gradually shifts to students while the teacher continues to provide guidance, explanations, and feedback. Students begin recording their thinking with sticky notes, T-charts, or learning logs.

Writing ideas are provided in each chapter to extend the lesson and to apply student learning. As students extend their thinking through writing, they become more conscious of the strategy and the content they are learning. In addition, they are further developing the language and thinking that are necessary for effective use of the strategy.

I recommend teaching only a few strategies and teaching them well—using anchor charts, the GO! Chart, and other tools described earlier in the chapter. The intention is to move students from understanding a skill (shared read-aloud) to applying it at a strategy level (guided practice). A skill has the potential to become a strategy only after students have been given many opportunities to practice the skill in many different contexts.

Assessing the Strategy: Behaviors to Look for in Student Reading and Writing

Assessment should always inform instruction. As you assess students' use of the strategy, you learn whether students are ready to begin applying the strategy on their own or whether they need more support from you. Assessment reveals misunderstanding or confusion about the strategy or the new information. It provides insight into how children are accessing, evaluating, and using information. Most important, it helps us to know if our strategy instruction is working.

The difficulty with assessing cognitive strategies is that they are invisible. How and what do you assess? In her book, *Teaching for Deep Comprehension,* Linda Dorn and Carla Soffos (2005) say that although reading strategies are invisible and cannot be observed, "they can be inferred by studying reading behaviors" (p. 40). Chapters 4 through 8 provide ideas for assessing each strategy with observation sheets and checklists that spell out behaviors to look for as students are trying out each strategy.

Assessment should also include self-reflection so students can evaluate how well the strategy helped them learn the new information. Students must know that the strategy is working. As a class, list what students learned about the strategy. Summarize the important aspects of the strategy with the students, have them put into their own words how they will use that strategy. Then create a wall chart students can refer to as they apply the strategy more independently.

Closing Thoughts

Although this chapter emphasized the tools, texts, and contexts for strategy instruction, remember these are a means to an end. The Go! Chart isn't the end result, and neither are learning logs. The strategies in themselves aren't even the final destination. They are simply ways to help students create understanding of information.

Information literacy requires multitasking—we must teach both cognitive strategies and content. In other words, we want students to use cognitive strategies *to gain a better and deeper understanding of the information* that they are reading—to become information literate. Each strategy must be applied to content to be useful (Duffy, 1993, 2002; Glaser, 1989; Pressley et al., 1992). You can learn to use a hammer and have it on hand and available. However, it isn't valuable until you need to hammer a nail into wood! So although you may incorporate these instructional strategies into your literacy block or use them with shared read-alouds, they should always have relevance for students in light of learning content information.

The teachers at Mandeville Elementary, for example, develop units of study at each grade level based on their state benchmarks. Then, as they plan their lessons, they incorporate a GO! Chart each week into their curriculum to teach part of their content. Each of the ideas and suggestions throughout this book become part of their instruction to help students learn about ladybugs, wetlands, communities, or the rainforest. And as their students are learning content, they are learning how to access, evaluate, and use the information. Is it cognitive strategy instruction? Yes. Is it content instruction? Yes. It is information literacy: teaching information with literacy and teaching literacy with information.

CHAPTER 4

Predicting to Access Information

❝I think that a robin laid those eggs," speculated second grader Marissa. We were looking at a photograph of a nest from the informational text *Eggs and Baby Birds* (Shirley, 1993).

"What makes you say that?" I asked her.

"Well, because I have a crayon in my box called 'robin's egg blue,' so that must be the color of the robin's egg."

"Wow!" I exclaimed. "You just did what good readers do. You took what you know about your crayon colors to figure out what kind of bird laid these eggs." Soon other students were sharing their stories about eggs, birds, and matters related to them.

The conversation held them captive throughout the reading. "When can we read the rest of the book?" George asked at the end of the lesson. "I want to know about other kinds of eggs. And we didn't find that out yet."

This group of second graders experienced the power of predicting—starting with Marissa predicting that a robin laid the eggs shown in the photograph. That initial prediction energized the classroom. While I guided the conversation that followed, she and her classmates were able to make connections to prior knowledge, find the language to discuss the new information, and wonder about other things related to birds and nesting.

When we predict, we think about what we are about to read in relation to what we already know. We connect the topic at hand to our prior knowledge. We speculate about what the author is going to tell us. Predicting is a prereading *access ramp* to the new information—it builds a ramp between what students know and what they seek to know.

The Strategy of Predicting: An Overview

In his book *Information Anxiety 2*, Richard Wurman and his coauthors (2000) identify a basic rule for successfully navigating information: You only learn something relative to something you already understand. Research confirms that comprehension is about linking what you already understand to what you want or need to know, making connections between the new information and your prior knowledge or personal experiences (Caine & Caine, 1991; Gordon & Pearson, 1983; Hansen, 1981; Kintsch, 1998; Pearson et al., 1992; Vockell, 1995).

Children must learn how to find and make these connections in order to begin to understand the new information. These connections help them focus, prepare to learn, and set a purpose for reading. Connections provide a "hook on which to hang the new information," as Walter Kintsch (1998) says. "Learning is most successful when such hooks are plentiful and when there is a clear relation between the hooks and the learning materials so that the student hangs things on the right hook" (p. 330). By encouraging children to predict what they are about to read or hear read to them, we help them forge those connections.

As Marissa, George, and the other second graders discussed birds and nesting, they were finding the hooks for the new information and, in the process, a purpose for reading. I guided that process with conversation.

VICKI:	Does this nest look the same as the nest with the blue eggs?
HANK:	No.
KYLEE:	It's upside down!
TYRONE:	Look, the bird has to go in from the bottom.
SARAH:	It's a different kind of bird.
VICKI:	What makes you say that, Sarah?
SARAH:	Different birds make different kinds of nests.
GEORGE:	They lay different kinds of eggs, too.

Dialogues like this move students beyond being curious about new information to comprehending new information. They give students the language, resources, and thinking tools they need during reading (Caine & Caine, 1991).

Reading researcher Doug Hartman (1994) contends that reading is "an open, on-going series of connections." He says, "Prior knowledge is not solely something readers bring to the passage and unload before they read. Rather . . . it is something utilized, constructed, and reconstructed by readers throughout reading" (p. 634). The reader accesses prior knowledge during reading in order to make sense of the new information.

A Mind Picture for Predicting

In order to help young readers predict what they'll learn from informational text, I use a metaphor—or, as I tell the children, a "mind picture"—of a weather forecaster. I ask, "How do you think the weather forecaster on TV knows what the weather is going to be tomorrow? How can she forecast a week in advance that it's going to be rainy, sunny, or cloudy?" We talk through the possible answers; I lead children to see that the weather forecaster doesn't actually just make up the weather (although sometimes it does seem that way!). Her forecast is an educated guess, based on her knowledge about climate, her ability to read weather instruments, her observations about weather patterns, and her past experiences forecasting the weather. She puts all that information together to anticipate the kind of weather that most likely will occur.

My students and I then talk about how a good reader's thinking is similar to a weather forecaster's, and we chart the comparisons.

Weather Forecasters:	Good Readers:
◆ look for clues in the weather from their maps and instruments, then think about what those clues tell them	◆ look for clues about the information on the outside and inside of the book, thinking about what they already know about the topic
◆ observe the weather closely	◆ think about what they have noticed and observed about the topic
◆ consider past experiences when they have seen those same patterns, or clues	◆ think about their own experiences or things they have read or seen on TV about the topic
◆ ask themselves what the clues and patterns might mean this time	◆ wonder about the things they have observed, read, or experienced, asking "Why" or "How"
◆ know how to look in more than one place for information about the weather	◆ know that there is more than one place in a book that offers clues, so they use text features and visuals as well as the title and cover
◆ know how to interpret the information from the instruments	◆ know how to think through the clues on the cover, in the text features, and in the visuals in order to look for connections
◆ put all their thinking together to make a forecast of the weather	◆ think about their connections from the clues and forecast different kinds of information that might be in the text

This mind picture helps children understand the work of predicting—forecasting based on an educated guess. A good predictor of informational text takes clues from the text and makes connections to his inner and outer worlds to anticipate what kind of information might be in the text.

Teaching Predicting: A Way to Introduce and Develop the Strategy

Children usually need help in learning how to think ahead to the new information. They will also need language to think about the new information during reading. The suggestions in this section will help you provide both, using the following teaching tools, which were introduced in Chapter 3:

- Tools for making thinking explicit: think-alouds, modeling, and explanations

- Tools for organizing and recording thinking: anchor charts, GO! Charts, sticky notes, and learning logs

- Tools for developing, guiding, and focusing talk: group conversations and pair and share

During the predicting conversation, it is important to show students how good readers get ready to learn new information by thinking ahead to the new information, or predicting. In the following sections, I explain how I worked with these second graders to develop their predicting skills and language, using the book *Eggs and Baby Birds* (Shirley, 1993). Specifically, I show you how I helped them to get ready to read by:

- Developing predictions about the new information

- Developing vocabulary for the new information

As students predict, they are:

→ Thinking about what they know

→ Thinking ahead to the new information

→ Focusing thinking

→ Saying their thinking out loud

→ Becoming aware of their thinking

→ Developing language to deal with the new information

→ Learning to multitask between the known and the new

Developing Predictions About the New Information

The objective of this 10- to 15-minute conversation with the class is to establish enough connections to create a list of predictions about the new information. These will be recorded on an anchor chart or in the first column of the GO! Chart. (See Chapter 3 for an explanation of the GO! Chart.) Use the following steps as a road map to guide the conversation:

+ Begin with the title or heading.

+ Take a picture talk.

+ Ask wondering questions.

+ Decide which chunk of text you will read.

+ Record predictions about the topic.

+ Pair and share prior knowledge and predictions.

Begin With the Title or Heading

This step probably seems too obvious. However, we have modeled reading aloud stories to children for so long that most children (and many teachers) automatically start reading information at the running text. I explain that good readers always begin at the beginning—and the beginning of informational text is always the title of the piece or heading of the section to be read. Drawing children's attention to the title emphasizes that all the information in the book will be connected to the text's big idea or main concept. All predicting is then focused toward the big idea reflected in the title or heading.

I think out loud about how the title helps readers to think ahead to the kind of information that most likely will be in the text.

VICKI:　　When good readers pick up an informational text, they always read the title to make sure they know what the text will be about. And like those weather forecasters, we learn to look for clues that tell us what kinds of information we can usually expect in a book like this. So the first place I look when I pick up an informational book is the title. Let's look at the title of our book today: [Reads with class] *Eggs and Baby Birds*.

Good readers try to figure out what kind of information will be in the book so that they can get their mind ready to learn the new information.

After the think-aloud, I model sharing what I know about the topic or have experienced. This gives children an entry point to begin thinking about their own experiences. Once they "see" my connection, it gives them a place to begin thinking about their own connections. The think-aloud jump-starts their thinking.

VICKI: Good readers think about what they already know when they look at the title. And so I think about the times that I have seen eggs or baby birds and what I know about them. I remember watching the baby chicks hatch out of their eggs one time at the state fair. Those baby birds didn't have nests because they were in an incubator. But I notice that these baby birds on the cover are in their nest. I wonder why nests are so important. Why did they have those eggs in incubators at the fair? What do you think?

At this point, children are invited to join in, allowing me to assess their prior knowledge and language as they participate. As they share, it provides the information that I need to build the access ramp to the new information for the students.

TYLER: To keep them warm.

MARISSA: They were away from their mama.

VICKI: So you are thinking that the incubator was like a nest? Tell me, have you seen baby birds or eggs in nests?

Several hands go up in our classroom to share their thinking and their stories about birds, nests, and eggs. The predicting conversation has begun.

Take a Picture Talk

To get the conversation going and invite everyone to participate, we take a "picture talk," an informal conversation based on photos or pictures in the book. The purpose is to talk about what we observe in the pictures, what we know about the topic, and experiences we've had that are related to it.

Predicting information is a bit more difficult than predicting story. Children sometimes have difficulty talking about prior knowledge or experiences. Some may not have learned how to tap their connections or

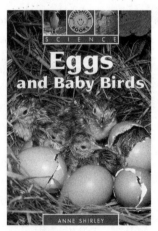

Vicki used the cover of *Eggs and Baby Birds* (Shirley, 1993) to begin the predicting conversation.

talk about their connections. Others may not yet have had experiences with the concept being learned. So, as we talk, I draw attention to the photo or picture to help draw out connections to prior knowledge and language about the topic that will help children make predictions.

VICKI:	Good readers look at the pictures in order to help them think about what they already know about the topic. We can take a "picture talk" to help us think about what *we* know. What do you think a picture talk might be?
RAPHAEL:	You look at the pictures.
KYLEE:	It's like a picture walk.
VICKI:	That's right! But what about that second part—a picture *talk*? What does that tell you?
LENI:	You talk about the picture.
JENNA:	Tell what you see. It's true.
VICKI:	Ah, that's important! So there are two things that will help us to think about what we know. First, we look closely at the picture, and second, we talk about what we observe. But as we talk, we want to remember what we are reading about. [Points to the title]
CLASS:	Eggs and baby birds.
VICKI:	So let's take a close look at the picture on the cover. Tell me what you notice about the eggs and baby birds on the cover.

A picture talk is a variation of the familiar strategy of a picture walk (looking through the pictures before reading). However, picture walks are traditionally associated with stories. I choose to use the term "picture talk" to identify it for children as a pre-reading strategy associated with informational text. Children use it to gather information, ask questions, develop topic-related language, and share connections for predicting information rather than talking about characters and what might happen in the story.

As discussed in Chapter 2, children need experiences first and then language to attach to those experiences to develop understanding. Photos can act as triggers for making connections to experiences. They are concrete artifacts upon which children can build their new understanding of the information. Even children with limited or no experience with the topic can describe what they see, ask questions, and wonder about the content.

The following sections give ideas to help children tap the power of a picture talk to develop both language and thinking for predicting information.

Encourage Elaboration During the Picture Talk Often in the beginning of strategy instruction, students' conversational responses are limited. Encourage children to elaborate as they observe visuals. Have students closely observe the picture. I use the phrase, "What do you notice?" to focus children's attention and encourage elaboration.

VICKI:	Let's look at this nest. What do you notice about it?
KYLEE:	It has eggs.
HANK:	With birds.
VICKI:	What else can you tell me? Look carefully at the picture. What do you notice about the baby birds?

Encourage children to observe carefully and describe photos for predicting.

Developing observation skills not only helps students to predict, but it also helps them meet important literacy benchmarks for most state standards. And as children learn to observe, they learn to express themselves.

VICKI:	What do you notice about where these baby birds are?
TYLER:	In their nest.
JOSÉ:	I don't see a nest.
HANK:	Just grass.
VICKI:	So you think the nest might be made out of grass?
SARAH:	No, it's straw.
GEORGE:	Straw is just grass.
VICKI:	So do birds just lay eggs in the grass?
GEORGE:	No! They have to put them in a nest.
VICKI:	So let's think. Where do you think this nest is—even if we can't see it?
KYLEE:	In a tree.

TYLER:	In the backyard.
JAMAL:	I saw one in my backyard!

I guided the children through a picture talk with a couple of key photos I chose in advance that would help them to compare and contrast the different nests.

VICKI:	Look at this picture. What do you notice about this nest?
TYLER:	I can't see it.
GEORGE:	I know, I know! There.
VICKI:	Where is the nest?
MARISSA:	There it is.
TYLER:	I can't see it.
KYLEE:	I found it.
SARAH:	Look, it's in the middle of the plant.
VICKI:	How is that nest different from the other nest we saw?
GEORGE:	This one is in a plant and the other was in a tree.
TYLER:	It's hard to see.
KYLEE:	They will get stuck if they try to get the nest.
VICKI:	Who will get stuck?
GEORGE:	The predators.
MARISSA:	That's because it's in a cactus and they hurt.
TYLER:	And it's camouflaged.

The picture talk opened the door for these second graders to observe various birds' nests, to compare them, and to begin to make their own connections. Tyler was able to see that the bird's nest was camouflaged by a plant. Kylee knew it was a prickly plant but she didn't know what it was called, and Marissa contributed the name of the plant: *cactus*. The picture talk allowed them to talk about what they knew as they discussed what they observed in the photos.

Teaching the Information Generation

Facilitate Connections During the Picture Talk As children begin to talk about the pictures, they move easily into sharing prior knowledge and experiences. Remember, predicting requires using what you know to anticipate what might be in the text. However, children often do not know that they know something. Laura Robb reminds us that as teachers we have to help students to "reclaim prior knowledge" that may have been hidden to them (2003). So it is important to listen to the conversation and let children know when they have made a connection.

Photos can help children access prior knowledge that they need to predict.

VICKI:	What do you notice about the nest in this picture? Does it look like the other nests that we saw?
JEROME:	That looks like a raccoon built that one.
VICKI:	Jerome, tell us what you know about raccoons that made you think that.
JEROME:	I don't know nothing about raccoons.
VICKI:	I bet you do know about them! You told us this nest looked like a raccoon built it. How did you know it looks like a raccoon might have made it?
JEROME:	It's on the ground, like a raccoon makes.
VICKI:	So you know that raccoons build their homes on the ground? How did you know that?
JEROME:	Hm-mm. Me and my dad go huntin'.

Jerome was not aware that he made a connection between what he was learning about birds' nests and what he knew about raccoons. The visual and the conversation allowed him to reclaim that prior knowledge and to help us in our discussion of looking at why birds build nests.

VICKI:	So you are thinking that some birds build nests on the ground just like a raccoon. I wonder why this bird built its nest there.
JEROME:	That way nothing can eat it.
VICKI:	You mean the eggs?
GEORGE:	They can't find them.
JEROME:	Predators can't eat the eggs.
MIKE:	To hide the eggs from snakes.
JEROME:	Yeah, snakes are predators.
VICKI:	So you think some of the nests are built to hide the eggs?

Jerome moved the discussion beyond describing the nests to looking at the reasons why birds build nests. He drew on his prior knowledge about raccoons and predators to help the rest of the class think about why the nest was on the ground.

Push students to think about where they have seen or experienced the phenomena in the real world. Kindergarten teacher Andie Cunningham (Cunningham & Shagoury, 2005) contends that we miss a step with young children and comprehension by not teaching them *self-to-text connections* first before learning to make text-to-self connections. Children must learn to bring themselves to the text before they can connect to the new information.

Keep the Conversation on Topic and on Task During the Picture Talk Most primary teachers know that when children begin sharing their stories, they have a hard time stopping! So it is our job to keep the conversation guided and focused on the new information—on topic and on task.

Children often need to be guided back to the title or heading when they start veering from the big picture. For example, during my lesson, some of the boys became fascinated by the picture of the nest on the ground, the one that Jerome said looked like a raccoon had built. So it was important for me to refocus them on the topic at hand—bird nests—so they would be tuned in to the information as they read.

STEVE:	I think it looks like a snake's nest.
MIKAL:	Yeah, snakes have to live there. It's on the ground.
VICKI:	But let's remember what we are reading about. Let's go back to our heading. Read it with me.
CLASS:	Why birds build nests.

VICKI:	Are we reading about snakes?
CLASS:	No. [Different responses about birds or nests]
VICKI:	So what are we reading about here?
CLASS:	[Various responses about bird nests]
VICKI:	So let's go back and look at this picture again. What do you notice about this nest?
MIKAL:	It's a snake nest.
VICKI:	Remember, what are we reading about?
STEVE:	It looks like a snake lives there.
MIKAL:	Gotta be a snake.

As I redirected them back to the title for the third time, Kylee turned to another teacher sitting on the floor next to her and whispered, "They just don't get it, do they?" Kylee knew that it didn't make sense to have a picture of a snake's nest in the section about birds! However, for others, it took repeated redirecting to keep them focused on the topic at hand.

I tell children that they want to be on the same channel as the author when they read, and predicting can ensure that. It is important for them to understand that if they are thinking about snakes as they read and the author is telling them about birds' nests, it will be hard for them to remember and understand the information. Before reading, good readers tune into the same channel as the author.

Ask Wondering Questions

Good readers ask questions they want answered in the text. They wonder. However, as Stephanie Harvey states in *Nonfiction Matters* (1998), it is difficult to wonder about something you know nothing about. Once children establish some knowledge about the topic, they are far more likely to wonder about it. During the picture talk, model how to ask wondering questions. Turn students' noticings into wonderings.

VICKI:	So let's think. Where do you think this nest is—even if we can't see it?
KYLEE:	In a tree.
TYLER:	In the backyard.
JAMAL:	I saw one in my backyard!

VICKI: I wonder in what kinds of places birds build nests.

As we talked about the photo of the nest in the cactus, I said, "I wonder why birds would build nests in a cactus." And after the discussion about the photo of the nest on the ground: "I wonder which bird builds a nest on the ground. I wonder why they would need to build one there. Why didn't they build it in the tree?" I pepper the conversation with many wondering questions like those. As children hear wondering questions, they think and converse more freely. And soon they begin to ask their own wondering questions.

Decide Which Chunk of Text You Will Read

It is important for children to know that we don't have to read informational texts from beginning to end, like stories. We can read it in chunks, or bits and pieces, for the information we need. Reading in chunks helps us to process information more effectively as we allow the brain time to process the information before reading more.

So, to build that awareness, I choose only a section of the text to read for the lesson. I model how to use the table of contents to guide the students to that section.

VICKI: We've been looking at pictures of nests and comparing how they are different. But let's look at our title again, *Eggs and Baby Birds*. Did you notice that there is nothing in the title about nests! Why do you think that is?

TAQUITA: They're *in* the nests.

SARAH: That's their home.

VICKI: If we are going to find out about nests, let's see where we might start reading, because in an information book we don't have to start at the beginning. We can go right to the information that we need. Put your thumbs up when you hear a section that might have the information we need about nests. Let's read:

- Eggs and Baby Birds
- Why Do Birds Build Nests?
- Whose Nest?
- How Do Birds Build Nests?
- Eggs
- Incubating the Eggs
- Hatching
- Baby Birds

We talked through the various options, narrowing them down to sections about nests. Then we chose the section about why birds build nests.

Of course, if the book has no headings, you can read the entire text looking for specific kinds of information. Just don't overwhelm students with too much information. Determine chunks to read beforehand and break the text down for young readers. Then focus the predicting conversation toward the specific chunk of information.

Record Predictions About the Topic

By recording predictions during a picture talk, we summarize the conversation and allow children to see their thinking in real time. Predictions are recorded in the first column of the GO! Chart (see Chapter 3 for a further explanation of the GO! Chart). List the kinds of information students feel might be included in the book or section of the book that you plan to read.

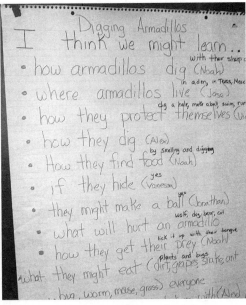

Here are some first-grade predictions about armadillos.

KYLEE:	I was thinking . . . that maybe if there are different nests that maybe we can figure out which birds go with what nests.
VICKI:	That's good, Kylee. So let's write down your thinking because I heard your thinking and I want you to see it. [Records prediction in the first column of the GO! Chart]
VICKI:	So you are thinking that we might learn what kinds of birds might build these different kinds of nests, is that right? [Talks out loud while writing "We might learn about which kind of birds . . ."]
GEORGE:	Make certain nests.
VICKI:	Make certain nests, you said? Because all of those nests didn't look the same, did they?

NICKY:	And some birds might go in other birds' nests and lay their eggs.
VICKI:	So you are thinking that not all birds make nests, Nicky?
NICKY:	No.
KYLEE:	Or if the birds leave their nests and decide to go somewhere else, then there will be that house. The nest will just be there.
VICKI:	So is your prediction that we might find out which birds build a nest and which ones borrow a nest?
GEORGE:	Maybe we should also figure out which birds come from, like, which eggs.
VICKI:	Another good prediction. Let's write down George's thinking.

Pair and Share Prior Knowledge and Predictions

To wrap up the predicting conversation, allow children opportunities to "pair and share" with their neighbors. Have children pair up and share what they know about the topic or what kind of information they think might be in the text. Children are sometimes more willing to share with a friend rather than in a group, and *all children* need the opportunity to talk about their thinking at this point.

As children participate in conversations like these, they learn to think about titles, headings, and pictures and talk through their connections to make predictions. They are learning to preview the text. Linda Dorn and Carla Soffos (2005), in their book *Teaching for Deep Comprehension*, explain that this is "central to learning." They observe, "Readers who lack the ability to preview texts for meaningful connections are likely to have impaired comprehension" (p. 43). The time spent on teaching children how to predict is time well invested.

Developing Vocabulary for the New Information

After predicting information, spend a few minutes before reading the text to develop vocabulary. This allows time and opportunity to expand language while continuing to expand prior knowledge. A great way to engage students with vocabulary is to first have them predict words they think the author might use to tell about the information. Then introduce new words they will actually encounter in the text.

Predict Known Vocabulary

After labeling the second column of the GO! Chart "Vocabulary," reread the predictions and have children think about words they already know about the topic. Then have them predict words that they might find in the reading, based on the earlier predicting conversation. Record the words in the second column.

This is a GO! Chart for developing vocabulary.

VICKI: You know all kinds of words about nests—I've heard some of them already. Let's write down some of the words that we think the author might use to tell about nests and why birds build nests. Let me show you.

I am thinking that we will probably find the word *protect* because we have talked about predators and it makes me think that would be a reason for the nest. What other words do you think about when you think of why birds build nests?

There are several advantages to having children predict vocabulary, which I discuss below.

Predicting Vocabulary Affirms That They Already Know Vocabulary Before They Read This is helpful to young readers, as the technical vocabulary that permeates informational text is often overwhelming. Assure them of how much they already know—doing so will increase comprehension. David Pearson (1993) contends that "the more one already knows, the more one comprehends; and the more one comprehends, the more one learns new knowledge . . ."

VICKI: Think about the nests that you've seen. What kinds of words might the author use to tell us about those nests?

STACY: Straw.

TAQUITA:	Grass.
JEROME:	Sticks.
VICKI:	It sounds like you are thinking about what they make these nests out of. Good thinking. [Charts *straw*, *grass*, and *sticks*] Do birds only make nests out of straw? What other words tell us what birds make nests out of?
GEORGE:	They could make them out of leaves.
KYLEE:	Flowers.
VICKI:	Have you seen a nest made with flowers?
KYLEE:	I saw a nest that had flowers in it.
MARISSA:	Four-leaf clovers.
HANK:	Cotton.
VICKI:	I wonder which of these the author will use in this section to tell us about why birds build nests.

Predicting Vocabulary Allows a Glimpse Into Children's Language By listening to children's predictions of vocabulary, you can assess how much language they have in their cognitive backpacks. Do they know labels (nouns)? What kind of technical vocabulary do they have about the subject? What misconceptions do they have? What kind of descriptive language do they possess (or need developed)? As Hank tried to add to our list, it gave me insight into his language. He knew the idea he wanted to share but just did not have the label for the word. I have to keep clarifying a child's thinking until we are both on the same page and I can offer the word he needs for his thought!

VICKI:	What words do you think might tell us what the nests will be made of?
HANK:	The stuff that hangs down from the trees.
VICKI:	Do you mean the branches, like in this picture of the nest hanging from the branch?
HANK:	No, the stuff that hangs on the branches. Like at the lake.
VICKI:	Do you mean moss? What hangs down from the trees?
HANK:	Yeah. Moss. Like at my grandma's.
VICKI:	Let's add *moss* to our list. Maybe birds that live around your grandmother's house use moss to build their nests.

Predicting Vocabulary Requires the Teacher to Focus Thinking So That Children Use Precise, Descriptive Language Children need an "entry point" for thinking about vocabulary words. It is too broad to ask children, "What kind of words do you think will be in this book?" Focus children's predicting by giving them a category of words.

VICKI:	I wonder if we will find out about the different places that birds build nests. What words might the author use to tell the location of different birds' nests?
GEORGE:	Like the branches in trees the birds will build their nests on.
VICKI:	So what if we add *branch* and *trees* to our list?
GEORGE:	I know those will be in there!
JEROME:	What about the ground? Like the nest that are like raccoons' nests.
VICKI:	Great thinking! I bet we might find different places that we don't usually think of for birds' nests. Let's add *ground*.

Predicting Vocabulary Prepares Students for Reading As children predict words that might be in the text, encourage them to talk through their thinking and connect their words back to the text's big idea, focusing thinking toward the new information.

VICKI:	Where else might birds build nests?
MIKAL:	Wal-Mart.
VICKI:	What makes you say a bird would build a nest in Wal-Mart?
MIKAL:	I saw one there before. He was flying around inside!
VICKI:	You are right! Sometimes birds build nests in buildings and outside buildings. So let's add *buildings* to our vocabulary list.
SARAH:	One time I found a bird inside the grocery store and people can't ever get it out, it's so high up. It's been living there for a year.
KYLEE:	And I saw one at the mall . . . [Hands go up all over the room!]
VICKI:	So let's look at our words up here. We have the word *buildings* and you guys have lots of stories where you've seen nests in different buildings. Turn and tell your neighbor about a time that you saw a nest in an unusual or strange spot.

Predicting Vocabulary Encourages Active Engagement During Reading When children predict a word, it becomes "their" word. They take ownership of the word and are ecstatic when it appears in the text. For example, Hank was excited to find that the hummingbird uses moss and spiderwebs to build its nest. I often hear, "The author used my word!" during reading.

Introduce New Vocabulary

Informational text contains technical vocabulary that is usually unfamiliar to young children. Traditionally, teachers have introduced that vocabulary before reading to increase comprehension during reading. However, that's risky practice because the brain is limited in terms of the number of unknown (or unconnected to prior knowledge) words it can hold. Research shows that the maximum number of words the brain can hold until they are processed is seven (Miller, 1956). Therefore, choose three to five vocabulary words that children will need most to comprehend the text.

I introduce the new words on the bottom part of the Vocabulary section of the GO! Chart. As I write each word on the chart, I pronounce it for children and then find out what they know (or think they know) about the new word. I ask children to rate themselves with a thumbs-up sign to find out their prior knowledge and experiences with each word. Then we talk through and share what they know about the word.

- Is this a word whose meaning you know?

- Is this a word that you have heard before but aren't quite sure what it means?

- Have you never heard this word before?

Reading research suggests that children learn most vocabulary instruction indirectly, that is, from hearing and seeing words used in many contexts (for example, conversations and reading). However, it also confirms that children need vocabulary instruction, including both word-specific instruction and strategic vocabulary instruction (*Report of the National Reading Panel,* 2000).

Word-Specific Instruction This type of instruction involves teaching individual words to increase student vocabulary and to increase comprehension of the new information. However, copying an unknown definition for an unknown word does not increase comprehension! Students need to be introduced to the meaning of an unfamiliar word within a context that they understand, and then they need repeated exposure to the new vocabulary word. The more they see the word and the more they use the word, the more likely they will learn the word.

Strategic Vocabulary Instruction This type of instruction provides strategies for solving an unknown word so that students will know what to do when they encounter new vocabulary and there is no teacher around. Rather than giving definitions for the new words, children clarify the meaning of the word as they read or after reading with teacher-guided discussion. This discussion emphasizes not only the meaning of the word, but the strategy for figuring out the meaning.

   ♦ Students look for clues *around the word*.

   ♦ Students use chunking strategies to look *inside the word*.

Further discussion about clarifying the meaning of words is in the following chapter in the section on guiding the reading of informational text (pages 82–94).

Reading the New Information

The reading of the new information is usually carried out on the same day as the prediction and vocabulary conversation. However, the focus of this chapter is on teaching students how to *get ready* to learn. Suggestions for guiding the reading of the information and confirming predictions is explored in the next chapter.

Trying Out Predicting: Ideas for Helping Students Apply the Strategy to Reading and Writing

As students become comfortable with predicting through conversations, they will need opportunities to try out the strategy. This guided practice allows young learners to develop the thinking and language necessary for predicting on their own, first with texts at their instructional level and eventually with texts that they choose.

Choosing Key Vocabulary

Laura Robb (2003) suggests asking these questions when selecting key words to introduce before reading:

→ Is the word necessary for students to comprehend the passage?

→ Is the word crucial to understanding the concept?

→ Has the author embedded a clear enough explanation of the term in the passage and/or illustrations?

Offering Guided Practice

Within the context of small groups or buddy reading, have students pair and share their predictions about an informational text. Students should take a picture talk with their partner and then discuss what kind of information they think will be in the text, sharing what they already know about the topic. When first shifting this responsibility to children, it might help to have them record their predictions on sticky notes and put them on the anchor chart. This allows the teacher to observe the predictions, offer feedback, and continue to guide thinking. As children become more able, they record their predictions in learning logs and then talk through their predictions with partners or the group. Debbie Stirling has her second-grade partners record "backpack knowledge" in their learning logs before they read.

Children can also record predicted vocabulary on sticky notes. After the picture talk and predicting conversation, children record two to four words that they predict the author will use. Sticky notes can be used to talk with partners or to bring the discussion back to the whole group as partners share their predicted words.

Providing Language Work

Language activities provide opportunities to "fill backpacks" with more descriptive language and prior knowledge for students who lack sufficient language and/or experiences for predicting. Here's an activity to try:

As you conduct the picture talk, help children brainstorm nouns, adjectives, verbs, or adverbs about the topic. As children volunteer words, record each one on an index card and place it in a pocket chart. (I find it helpful to color-code the words: i.e., blue for nouns, red for adjectives, green for verbs, etc.) These words will be used in a sentence frame to talk about the topic.

For example, in a first-grade classroom we were reading Joy Cowley's (2005) informational text, *Chameleon, Chameleon*. As we conducted a picture talk, we observed the wonderfully vivid photos of the chameleon in the book. I placed a sentence-strip frame in the pocket chart: The _____ chameleon _____. From looking at the photos, the class generated two lists: *what the chameleon looks like* and *what the chameleon does*.

After we generated 10 to 15 words in each list, I invited volunteers to come to the pocket chart to choose words from the word banks that would fit into the sentence frame. As Latoya placed her words into the frame, the entire class then read the sentence: The quiet chameleon sleeps. Then we checked to make sure that the sentence matched the picture that we were using by asking the following questions:

Teaching the Information Generation

- Does it make sense? (*Do the words match the photo?*)

- Does it sound right? (*Do the words go together grammatically?*)

It is important for children to have the opportunity to physically manipulate the language, allowing them to be kinesthetically and tactilely involved with their thinking. I usually allow six to eight volunteers to come up and try out the sentence frame, returning the words to the word banks to be used again.

This activity is used here to develop language for tapping prior knowledge and predicting. More language work is included in the following chapter for learning the new information.

Challenging More Proficient Readers

Rather than predicting from a picture talk, challenge more proficient readers by giving them a list of vocabulary words from the text and asking them to predict what the text is about. This also works well to extend student thinking when children have had multiple opportunities to predict through picture talks.

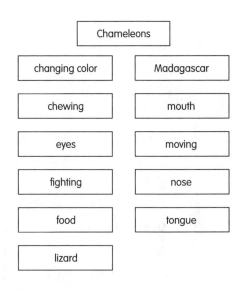

To do this, the teacher chooses six to ten words from the text that will help students to think about the concept. These are not intended to be the new technical vocabulary words, as discussed in the vocabulary section. Rather, these are words that will cause students to think about how the words might be related to the topic and how they give the reader clues about the information the author will share.

Beth had been predicting using the GO! Chart in her first-grade classroom successfully for a while. So to challenge her students, she pulled several words from the index to get them to think about the information about chameleons that might be in the informational text *Chameleons Are Cool* (Jenkins, 2001).

BETH: I opened our book *Chameleons Are Cool* to the back to get clues for our predicting, rather than using the picture on the front. The back is where the index is. Look at what's here. This gives me a list of important words in the book and then tells me what page I can find them on. I put these words on cards so that you can see them, since we know these are important words the author will use. The index can give us lots of clues! We're going to take these clues to make our predictions.

Beth read through the words with her students and then guided their predicting conversation. The words became the springboard for discussion.

BETH: Using these clues, what can we predict that the author might tell us in this nonfiction text?

JENNA: What chameleons eat.

BETH: What word gave you that idea?

JENNA: Food.

[Beth charts prediction]

JENNA: What do chameleons eat?

BETH: That's what we want to read to find out.

As children use a list of words to predict, it is important that they elaborate on the words and their thinking. Get them to talk through their connections.

BETH: What else do we think we might find out about?

DAKOTA: Where they live.

BETH: That's what the index tells us. How can that help us to think about what the author might tell us about where they live?

DAKOTA: Maybe in the forest or the jungle.

JASMINE: Some chameleons live in Australia.

CHASE: Some live here. They got one next door.

BETH: So I wonder if they live here in Louisiana. Do you see chameleons in your backyard?

DAKOTA: Maybe someone brought them from another country.

It is important that students be able to talk through their thinking and to relate the word, their thinking, and the prediction.

VICTOR: They live in Madagascar.

BETH: What makes you say that?

VICTOR:	Because it's up there.
BETH:	How did you know it was a place?
JASMINE:	Maybe it's the name of a tree.
VICTOR:	I know it's a place.
JENNA:	Maybe it's a state—
ZOE:	Or a country.
ISAAC:	Or a car.
BETH:	If it is a car, how would it relate to chameleons?
ISAAC:	I was just using the clue.
BETH:	Can we just use the clue? We have to think about the word as it relates to chameleons.

Predicting from text vocabulary is a great way to introduce students to the index and to use words from the index to focus predicting.

Assessing Predicting: Behaviors to Look for in Student Reading and Writing

In order to assess students effectively, listen to and observe closely what is said and done during predicting conversations. Listen to who is participating and watch for who isn't. Invite students who aren't participating to join in, and notice their response. Observe these children when they pair and share their predictions. Are they able to think

Behaviors to Look and Listen For

(Behaviors that indicate students are learning to think ahead to the new information)

→ Begins with title or heading

→ Talks through the photos and visuals to preview the text

→ Describes visuals

→ Makes connections to prior knowledge or experiences

→ Has sufficient language to talk through their thinking before reading

→ Shares their prior knowledge or experiences

→ Makes predictions about kinds of information

→ Writes predictions/write their thinking

→ Generates language/ words about topic

→ Uses logical thinking in making predictions

ahead to the new information? Are they able to share prior knowledge and connections? Do they have the language for sharing their thinking?

Checklists provide a written record of teacher observations. They can also provide students with a list of what they should be doing when predicting together. Before creating a checklist, I find it valuable to make a list with the students of the important things we want to remember when predicting. I guide students in creating a charted list of three to five things that include the expected behaviors that will be on their checklists. We hang the list on the wall so that all can see and know what the expectations are from the beginning.

Closing Thoughts

As students learn to predict, they begin to move toward thinking of information as being connected. Wurman (2000) confirms that this is how to navigate information to avoid information anxiety. He says, "Just as architecture is making connections—the way that two rooms are connected, the way a floor meets a wall, the way a piece of wood meets a piece of metal, the way a building meets a street—so is all learning." We must consider information as being connected, not as thousands of isolated facts.

When students know how to predict, they will soon anticipate these connections when they read an informational text. They will begin to embrace that, like architecture, all new information must be connected somewhere. And then the new information will be usable and accessible to them as information-literate students.

CHAPTER 5

Evaluating Text
for Literal Understanding

"**L**ook. My book has an index, a glossary, *and* a table of contents," announced Sharilyn when she returned from the library with the rest of her first-grade class. "Did you use any of those features to help you pick your book?" asked her teacher, Beth Laine.

"I was looking for more stuff about Chinese water dragons. First I looked at the table of contents, then I found the index. I looked up *dragon* and *chameleons* and then looked at each page to find a Chinese water dragon. I knew they were chameleons. So when I found a book with a Chinese water dragon in it, I got it!" Sharilyn was not only learning about chameleons, she was also learning how to find information in text.

Finding the information, however, is really just the initial step. A proficient reader also knows how to read informational text to *evaluate for literal understanding*. Finding the information is like getting to first base. Getting to second base requires knowing how to pull the facts from the text and making sense of them at a literal level. Getting to third base requires interpreting that information at a more critical level of thinking. The reader arrives at home base when she integrates new information from the text with prior knowledge to arrive at a higher level of understanding about the topic. These first graders hit a first-base run by using the features of informational text.

In this chapter, I explore how to help students get to "second base" with information literacy: evaluating informational text to establish a literal-level understanding about the topic. I discuss the theoretical underpinnings of the strategy, ways to teach it, ways to help students apply it independently, and, finally, ways to assess students to make sure they have a firm grasp on it. In the next chapters, I explore how to move students to "third base"—evaluating informational text to establish *critical and conceptual* levels of understanding about the topic.

The Strategy of Evaluating Text for Literal Understanding: An Overview

Literal understanding is the cornerstone of critical thinking. It is the foundation on which the reader will build her personal, dynamic understanding of the information. It is the point from which interpretations, connections, opinions, feelings, judgments, and beliefs about the information grow. It is recognizing ideas and facts explicitly stated in the text, as well as those implied.

Literal understanding starts with getting the facts, whether explicitly stated or inferred. For example, when discussing *Manatees and Dugongs* (Cole, 2000) in a third-grade classroom, José noticed that manatees are larger than dugongs.

VICKI:	José, how did you know that manatees were bigger than dugongs? How do we know that is a fact?
JOSÉ:	Look at the chart.
VICKI:	What page, José, so that everyone can look with you?
JOSÉ:	Right here on page 9. See the picture of the manatee? He is a whole lot bigger than the dugong, which is littler.
COURTNEY:	Yeah, the manatee is really fat.
VICKI:	What other facts do you notice about the manatee being larger, either from the chart, from the text that we read, or from your figuring things out?
BRIAN:	The manatee weighs 2,900 more pounds than the dugong.
VICKI:	Wow! How did you figure that out? The chart doesn't tell us.
BRIAN:	It says the manatee weighs 3,500 pounds and the dugong weighs 600. So you just do the math.

Learning Behaviors That Demonstrate Literal Understanding

→ Observing

→ Describing

→ Listing

→ Showing

→ Labeling

→ Paraphrasing

→ Comparing

→ Contrasting

→ Inferring

→ Explaining

(Based on Bloom's taxonomy, 1984)

Teaching the Information Generation

The author established the fact that manatees are larger than dugongs. We could prove it by comparing photos and weights. Sometimes we find the information in the running text, sometimes in the access features, and sometimes the reader must infer, as José and Brian did. Reading information for literal understanding requires up-and-down and back-and-forth kinds of reading. Helping students use access features to find information and then evaluate it is one of the keys to helping them learn to create literal understanding.

The strategies in this chapter will help children pull out facts for literal understanding to:

- Read the layout up and down, back and forth

- Chunk information

- Interpret access features

- Connect visuals to information

- See relationships between pieces of information

- Describe the information, both when it's explicitly stated and when it's implied

A Mind Picture for Evaluating Text for Literal Understanding

I use what is most primary students' all-time favorite meal, macaroni and cheese, as a mind picture to help children understand about how to read informational text to evaluate. Specifically, I ask them to tell me what they notice about the macaroni-and-cheese box and what it says. Typical responses include, "It tells you what to make" and "It shows you the picture of what it's supposed to look like." I ask, "What other information does the box tell you?"

I guide them to see that there are different kinds of information on the different sides of the box (ingredients, nutritional information, pictures, offers, recipes, directions). I show them how I have to look in different places to find the information, since it isn't all in one place. "Do I have to read all this information?" I ask. I share with them that, in all the times I have made macaroni and cheese, I have only read what I needed or wanted to know.

I want students to see that information is read in a less linear manner than stories. As a proficient reader, I might read a bit of the text, then check out the graphics, going back to the text to clarify the graphic or use the graphic to clarify a point in the text. Indeed, reading an informational text is a bit like reading the box of macaroni and cheese—up and down, back and forth. As we talk, I chart key points (see page 80) so that children can see how thinking of a box of macaroni and cheese can help them to think about how to read informational text.

Macaroni and Cheese	Informational Text
◆ The box makes you want to eat the macaroni and cheese because of the pictures and interesting stuff on the box.	◆ Informational text has lots of pictures that make you want to read the information because it looks interesting.
◆ It tells you on the front of the box what is in the box so that you know what you are going to make.	◆ The title and heading tell you what kind of information is in the text so that you know what kind of information to think about.
◆ It tells you on the front if it's microwaveable or regular so you know how to make it.	◆ The layout of the book usually gives you clues about, whether it's fiction or nonfiction, so that you know how to read it.
◆ It shows you a picture of what it should look like.	◆ Nonfiction gives you lots of pictures so that you can see what the author is talking about.
◆ Most of the ingredients are in the box, but you still have to provide the milk and butter yourself.	◆ Good readers know to get the facts from the book, but they also have to bring their own connections to the facts.
◆ It gives you most of the stuff and tells you how to make it, but you have to mix it together to get macaroni and cheese.	◆ The facts are in the book, but you have to mix the facts with your thinking and your connections to understand it.
◆ You find which information that you need or want to read on the box. Some people might read the ingredients first, and others might read the directions.	◆ People read different information depending on the information they are looking for. Some people read the picture first, and some read the words first.
◆ There are directions on the side of the box to tell you how to make macaroni and cheese.	◆ When we are learning how to read information, it helps to have directions.
◆ Once you learn how to make macaroni and cheese and you make it lots of times, you don't need to read the directions anymore.	◆ Good readers know how to read information and don't need directions about how to read it because they already know what to do.

Teaching the Information Generation

As we talk, I tell kids that I have made lots of macaroni and cheese over the years, and I ask them if I need the directions on the side. "But if you are learning to make macaroni and cheese, wouldn't it be helpful to follow these directions over and over until you learn how to make it?" And they all agree. Of course, they could figure it out on their own, but it would be so much easier following the directions—that's why they are on the outside of the box.

From there, I pick up their science book, turn it over, and ask, "Are there directions on how to read this science book?" I let children know that since I have read lots of informational text (like making lots of macaroni and cheese), I am going to help them by writing out the directions for how to read it themselves. We chart the steps (which are explained in the following section). Over the course of the following weeks, we refer to these steps as I introduce and develop the strategy of evaluating informational text for literal understanding.

Teaching Evaluating Text for Literal Understanding: A Way to Introduce and Develop the Strategy

Beth was reading a book about farms to her first graders as part of a unit on that topic. As she read she talked through the text with her students, moving between the running text and the visual on the page. "Look at this photo the author put on this page. It says in the caption that this is an oyster farm. Now I wonder why the author put a picture about an oyster farm on this page. Tell me, what do you think?"

The first graders all chimed in and offered their thoughts: "Maybe it's a kind of a farm." "I didn't know they grow oysters on farms." "How can you have oysters on a farm? They live in the ocean!"

After revisiting the running text, the students noticed that the author did not talk about oyster farms. "So why do you think the author put this picture here? How does it help us to think about farms?" Beth asked.

The children answered, "I know! It's a kind of a farm." "There are lots of different kinds of farms." "Some are special farms." "You grow things on a farm, and he grows oysters."

While watching and listening to Beth and her first graders, I realized what a far cry this was from reading aloud stories to children. In fact, it was a far cry from the typical reading of informational text: a straight-through, uninterrupted reading with "comprehension" questions at the end. This was a wonderful balance of a little reading, a little looking, a bit of talking, and a lot of thinking.

In this section I suggest ways to show children how to evaluate for literal understanding, referring to the teaching tools introduced in Chapter 3:

- Tools for making thinking explicit: think-alouds, modeling, and explanations
- Tools for organizing and recording thinking: anchor charts, GO! Charts, sticky notes, and learning logs
- Tools for talk: group conversations and partner sharing

Guiding Reading of Informational Text

Most children will come to you having little or no experience reading informational text for literal understanding. So initially, they need lots of modeling. The following section provides suggestions for making your thinking explicit, organizing and recording students' thinking, and facilitating the kinds of rich conversations described in Chapter 2. I present these suggestions in the context of a shared read-aloud, but they can also be used in small groups and with individual students.

Read Only a Bit of Information at a Time

In teaching students how to read informational text, choose to read only a short section of the text. Remember, too much information usually results in very little learning (Miller, 1956; Vockell, 1995). The brain needs time to process the new information and shift it from short-term memory to long-term memory (as discussed in Chapter 2), and children need time to develop the kind of thinking and language necessary to read, think about, and discuss informational text. Presenting them with only bits of information during shared read-aloud allows that.

Break the text down into sections with headings so that young readers can see how authors organize the information. When the text does not contain headings, chunk the information for students. For example, when reading *Bird Beaks* (Noonan, 1994), I chose to read and discuss only some of the birds, which are each presented on a different page. Although I teach only a bit of information at a time, I encourage students to stop, talk, and think deeply about those bits, and once I've read a complete section, I encourage students to make connections among the facts.

Talk About the Text as You Read

Talking is a critical part of processing information. So as you read, be sure to talk through the information. Elaborate on points that the author makes and on what you notice in the visuals. Don't be afraid to express what you're thinking. When we elaborate, we actually

Teaching the Information Generation

fill in details pulled from our prior knowledge. Elaborating also pushes children to put the information into their own words and expand on it.

José and Brian were learning to elaborate as they talked about their understanding of the manatee's size. They were able to take the graph in the book and fill in the details, comparing the manatee to the dugong and doing the math to figure out how much larger the manatee is.

Read Between the Visuals and the Text

Proficient readers of informational text read up and down and back and forth, moving between the headings, the text, and the visuals. In the beginning of the year, I explicitly teach this process following the steps outlined below. As children learn to read between the running text and the visuals, they learn to anticipate information in each of these locations—a critical step in creating literal understanding with informational text.

Laurie Castagna models how to read between a book's features and text for literal understanding.

Start With the Heading As discussed in Chapter 4, the beginning of predicting for informational text is always the title; and the beginning of reading the new information is to return to the heading or title before reading. This helps readers get their mind ready for the new information, focusing the thinking (remember that Information Generation children are scattered in their thinking), and reiterating that all the facts in the section (or chunk) will be connected to this topic.

1. Start with the heading.
2. Tell about the picture.
3. Think about the new information.
4. Read the text.
5. Look at the picture again.
6. Connect the picture to the text.

Tell About the Picture After beginning with the title or heading, direct attention to the picture or visual on the page for a mini–picture talk. The visual is a doorway for processing the new information and models the back-and-forth kind of reading good readers use. Steve Moline (1995) contends that visuals make the new information accessible to all students, regardless of their reading or language ability: "One of the greatest advantages of visual texts, such as maps or diagrams, is that most of the information they provide is readily accessible to all readers, including very young children who are not yet fluent readers of words and older students whose first language is not English" (p. 1).

Informational books for young readers mostly use photographs for visual access features. This is a perfect place to start modeling how to read between the visual access features and the running text, as photos are inviting and engaging to children. They will readily talk about the photo, allowing a more level playing field for students with limited experiences. As they talk, they are getting their mind ready for the new information.

VICKI: [Using *Eggs and Baby Birds*] Now let's turn the page. Before we read the words, though, we want to notice the picture. This will help us to get a picture in our mind as we read. I want you to first look at the picture. Closely observe the picture of the nest. Remember, we are thinking about why birds build nests. Tell me, what do you notice?

KENDALL: Baby birds.

MARISSA: Baby blackbirds.

VICKI: What else do you notice?

GEORGE: They're ugly.

NICKY: That's 'cause they're being born.

KYLEE: They look brand new.

Begin with the power of the picture and later introduce texts with other types of visual features. Children will need to learn to identify and use other visual features, such as maps, charts, and diagrams. But for this part of the conversation, I always try to find a photo or picture to start the text talk. As children share what they notice in the visual, an understanding conversation begins.

Think About the New Information As children are sharing, guide the conversation and thinking toward the new information, getting students to think about the picture in light of the topic. "How might this picture help us think about why birds build nests?" Children will offer what they already know, elaborating by filling in the details. This part of the conversation provides a bridge to the new information and allows insight into students' prior knowledge and misconceptions about the information.

I use this opportunity to gather information from the caption as well, showing children that this is a clue to the information. Children shift from "Do we have to read the caption?" to more eagerly looking for information in the caption.

VICKI: Kendall, how did you know these were blackbirds?

KENDALL: The caption.

Vicki:	What information does the caption tell us? Let's read it.
Class [reads]:	"Blackbird chicks in their nest."

Read the Text After reading the heading and having a brief conversation about the picture, it is time to read the running text for the new information. Our mind is ready and the pump is primed.

Vicki:	So let's read and see what the text tells us about why birds build nests. Do you think this is just going to be about the blackbirds and their nest?
Class:	No.
Kylee:	*All* birds.
George:	Maybe different kinds of birds and their nests.
Vicki:	So I have this question as I read: I wonder why the author put this picture here. How can this picture help me to create a picture in my head for this information? Let's think about that as we read.

Read only the page or short section. Then model how to "read a bit, stop a bit, think a bit, and talk a bit." Now is the time to stop and talk about the information in order to model how to think about the information (to evaluate for literal understanding). Students need to know that stopping and talking about the information will help them to better learn and remember the information.

Look at the Picture Again Returning to the picture provides a stimulus for thinking about the new information. This seems to help children create a conversation about the new information, inviting them to elaborate (fill in the details) and pushing them to put the information into their own words rather than spouting facts without thinking. This also emphasizes pulling information from the visual or photo when talking about the information.

Vicki:	Now the author just gave us four reasons why birds build nests. Let's go back to the picture and think about which reason it's showing.
Kylee:	You could say "stay in one place" because they are all right there.
Vicki:	They are in one place, right? So it's a way for me to see that when birds are born, they are all in one place. Why do you think they need to be in one place?

SARAH:	Keeping warm.
VICKI:	How are they keeping warm?
KYLEE:	They're all huddled together.
TYRONE:	Yeah, like football players.
VICKI:	Football players, huh? What makes you say that, Tyrone?
TYRONE:	They all scrunch up together.
HANK:	They get all close when they tell about the plays.
VICKI:	So you are thinking that the baby birds are all close? All scrunched up together, huh? Why are they huddling together, do you think?
TYLER:	To keep warm. You're warm when you're close.
VICKI:	And that is part of the information that the author gave us. Let's look back and read that information again.

Connect the Picture to the Text Children need to learn how to interpret not only maps and diagrams, but photos as well. Too often children "read" through an informational book looking only at the pictures. They are engaged and engrossed in the photo, but do not necessarily think about the photo in relationship to the information.

To be information literate, children need to learn to describe the photo and then to think about the photo in light of the information in the text. Sometimes there is new information in the visuals. The connection, or relationship, between the visual and the information in the running text is often not explicitly stated, but must be inferred. The reader must think "between facts" to infer the connection. Our young readers learn that sometimes authors only tell us part of the information, or give us clues about the information. The reader must figure out in his head how the access feature is related to the information. This is especially critical with today's more complex text layouts, as discussed in Chapter 2.

Talking through the connection will also bring to light children's misconceptions about the picture or the information. Without connecting the photo to the text or the concept, children may let their interpretations override the information, as with the bird's nest and Mikal's insistence that it was a snake's nest (in Chapter 4).

Look for Other Access Features After talking through the new information with the photo, guide the conversation and reading from photos to other access features included in the section or on the page, such as maps, graphs, and diagrams. Use mini-lessons to

A large earthquake might have a **magnitude** (mag-nuh-*tood*) of 6.5 or 7 or even higher. The smaller ones have magnitudes of 2 or 3.

A scientist checks seismograph readings.

Scientists use special instruments called **seismographs** (size-muh-*grafs*) to measure the strength of an earthquake. They rate earthquakes on a scale. The higher the number, the stronger the quake.

Take a Closer Look

Seismograph reading from 1989's 7.1 magnitude earthquake near Loma Prieta Peak, in California

Guide children to consider how the visuals relate to the text.

teach the different purposes of access features as they occur during the reading. Be sure to always associate the access feature with the information; it's not meant to be read in isolation.

> **VICKI:** I noticed that the author used bullets in the information on this page. That lets me know this is a list the author is giving us. And here is the first reason that birds build nests. [Points to the first bullet]

Birds build nests to

- protect the eggs from enemies
- keep eggs in one place for the parent to sit on and keep warm
- keep the eggs warm when the parents are away
- protect the baby birds when they hatch

> **VICKI:** What information did she tell us? How do the bullets help us when we read?

Connecting Access Features and Text for Literal Understanding

Questions to guide conversations:

➜ What is this (access feature)?

➜ What information does it give us?

➜ What do you think the author is telling us with this?

➜ Why did the author choose to use this feature?

➜ What does this tell us about the topic?

➜ How could you use it to help you learn about this information?

There are many different access features that authors use to present information. Some common features used in children's informational texts include maps, diagrams, charts, and graphs. Steve Moline's book *I See What You Mean* (1995) is an excellent resource for explanations and suggestions for these types of visual features.

Pair and Share the Information Provide opportunities for children to voice their understanding of the new information to a partner. They can describe the photo, retell the information on the page, tell how the access feature (such as bullets or a graph) helped them understand the information, or remark on something new that they learned. The more opportunities for social talk and conversations that children have, the more they develop cognitive language and inner conversations for reading.

VICKI: Turn and tell your neighbor about the graph of the manatee and dugong here on page 9. Look at the graph and then tell your partner in your own words all the information that this graph tells you. Be sure to tell it as if they have never seen the graph before.

Observe and Describe the Information

One of the purposes of explicitly guiding reading is to teach students how to focus their energy on noticing the important information that the author states or infers. From there, children need to learn how to describe what they notice.

Children need opportunities to talk through new information.

VICKI: What do you notice about the picture?

HANK: There's eggs.

TYLER: Birds.

Initially, describing information can be difficult for students. Teaching students to use decontextualized language and descriptive attributes makes it easier for them by giving them the vocabulary they need to describe what they notice.

Teach Students to Use Decontextualized Language To understand decontextualized language, we must first understand contextualized language. Most conversations—as well as question-and-answer sessions—use *contextualized* language, meaning that language is used within a context of meaning. Participants in the conversation are familiar with the context, and the conversation revolves around common understandings. Therefore, using contextualized language of pronouns makes sense. For example, in this case, everyone in the class had seen the picture of the birds in the nest. When the children participated in a conversation about the picture, it was natural to use pronouns to talk about the baby birds.

VICKI:	Look at the picture again of the nest. Tell me what is happening in this picture.
TYLER:	They're in the nest.

In fact, children have a lot more practice in using pronouns than nouns. Most conversations at home use contextualized language, and it is reinforced again at school with question-and-answer sessions. Children become accustomed to using contextualized language for most of their language interactions. However, when children have to retell information or write a written response, the expectation is to use *decontextualized* language, or nouns, to talk about the information.

During the understanding conversation, it is important to explicitly teach and emphasize the use of nouns when talking about the information. Therefore, the first step in teaching decontextualized language is to *label* the object (or person) the children see in the photo or that is discussed in the text. Make sure that students use the noun to refer to the *who* or *what* of the section in the conversation.

VICKI:	Look at the picture again of the nest. Tell me what is happening in this picture.
TYLER:	They're in the nest.
VICKI:	Who is in the nest? We need to tell who the picture is about.
MIKAL:	The birds.
SARAH:	The babies.
MARISSA:	Babies *and* eggs.
VICKI:	So this picture is about baby birds and eggs.

As you establish decontextualized language with this first step, you are also helping your young readers to do the following:

- Identify the subject and focal point for elaborating

- Focus reading energies

- Help keep the conversation on target

- Determine what's important to know

Teach Students to Use Descriptive Attributes Once children label the subject of the photo or information, they need language to describe the subject. Descriptive attributes are the distinguishing features or characteristics of what is being studied (such as size, shape, color, or location). Using descriptive attributes pushes children to look more carefully at the picture beyond their initial glance. It also teaches them how to elaborate, expanding thinking and language beyond simple statements such as "It's a bird" or "There's eggs."

Explain to students the importance of learning to observe as they read a bit, stop a bit, think a bit, and talk a bit.

VICKI: Scientists carefully notice things around them. They call this "observing." It's looking closely and carefully and thinking about what you notice. We are going to learn to notice as we read, and here are some ways that you can learn to notice so that you are observing like a scientist.

Introduce to students attribute categories to describe the subjects that they observe. Common types of attributes for describing concepts in most informational text include the following:

- Action: *What is it doing?*

- Size: *How big is it?*

- Shape: *What does it look like?*

- Location: *Where is it?*

- Colors: *What color is it?*

- Number words: *How many?*

- Material: *What is it made of?*

- Touch/texture: *What might it feel like?*

Use photos to teach descriptive attributes.

Teaching the Information Generation

I usually choose two or three attributes that best match the content. Then we make a list of those attributes for students to refer to during the conversation. Using the photo as a stimulus, I guide the conversation by asking questions that encourage students to brainstorm words that fit the attribute categories.

VICKI: How do you think that scientists tell which nests belong to which birds? When they observe a nest, they notice its size, shape, the materials the bird made it with, and where it was built—or its location. So today we are going to observe carefully when we read about bird nests. Remember good readers notice attributes. What are we looking for today? Size, shape, materials, and location.

One attribute that helps to kick off the conversation is the action attribute. Marcia Freeman (2000; 2003a) emphasizes using verbs for describing photos. She explains that using verbs helps children to better visualize by creating active, movie-type scenes in children's heads about the subject of the photo. I have found this to be true in teaching children how to observe and describe when reading for literal understanding. "What do you think is going on here?" or "Tell me what's happening in the picture" helps to get the reader actively involved and assists children in creating a mind movie for the action.

In the following conversation, I have labeled the attributes in order to illustrate how I used them to guide and shape the conversation. Here I was establishing how to observe a picture of babies in a nest, using action and number attributes.

VICKI: Look at the picture again of the nest. Tell me what is happening in this picture. (action attribute)

TYLER: They're in the nest.

VICKI: Who is in the nest? We need to tell who the picture is about. (subject)

MIKAL: The birds.

SARAH: The babies.

MARISSA: Babies and eggs.

VICKI: Now can you tell me, what do you think is happening in the nest? (action attribute)

MIKAL: They're hungry.

KYLEE: They're waiting on their mom to feed them.

VICKI:	What are these baby birds doing that makes you say they are hungry or waiting on their mom?
KYLEE:	Look at their mouths. They're open.
HANK:	They're stretching their necks.
VICKI:	Good noticing of the action! What number words can we use to tell about the birds or eggs? (*number attribute*)
TYLER:	Yeah, there are four birds.
KYLEE:	Four *babies*.
GEORGE:	One bird hasn't hatched all the way.
JOSÉ:	Two are cracked.
VICKI:	Two what are cracked, José?
JOSÉ:	Two eggs are cracked.
KYLEE:	That's cause they're being born!

Using attributes shifted the conversation from labeling to describing, as the children visualized what was going on in the nest. As children learn to first describe photos and then information using attribute language, they are learning to paraphrase. This is a beginning step to retelling information. It is also the foundation for literal understanding.

VICKI:	These are called attributes or characteristics. These are all the ways that you want to think when you notice. Think carefully when you read and pay attention to these attributes. These will help us to know how birds are alike and how they are different. How a woodpecker is like a robin but different. Because they do different things, they have different colors, shapes, and sizes. These are the thinking skills of both a scientist and a good reader. And that is what we are learning how to be.

During the understanding conversation, as the teacher guides the children to describe the photos, talk about the content, and discuss the big ideas, it is also important to model how to record information.

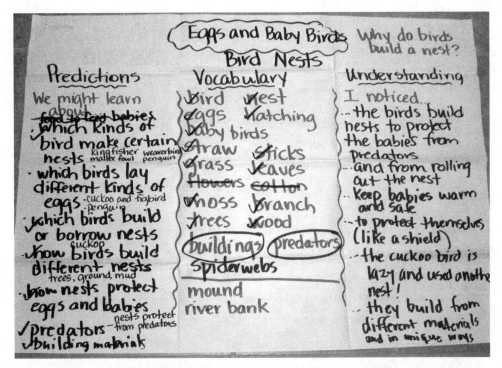

Eggs and Baby Birds   Why do birds build a nest?

Bird Nests

Predictions

We might learn
~~about~~ ~~food to feed babies~~
· which kinds of bird make certain nests ^King fisher weaverbird mallee fowl penguin
· which birds lay different kinds of eggs - cuckoo and frabird - penguin
· which birds build or borrow nests ^cuckoo
· how birds build different nests ^trees, ground, mud
· how nests protect eggs and babies ^nests protect from predators
✓ predators - from predators
✓ building materials

Vocabulary

✓bird ✓nest
✓eggs ✓hatching
✓baby birds
✓straw ✓sticks
✓grass ✓leaves
~~flowers~~ ~~cotton~~
✓moss ✓branch
✓trees ✓wood
(buildings) (predators)
spiderwebs
_____
mound
river bank

Understanding

I noticed...
·· the birds build nests to project the babies from predators
·· and from rolling out the nest
·· keep babies warm and safe
·· to protect themselves (like a shield)
·· the cuckoo bird is lazy and used another nest!
·· they build from different materials and in unique ways

This is the GO! Chart Vicki used to record information about bird nests.

Record Important Information You Notice

VICKI: Let's write down the facts that we noticed in this section about why birds build nests, because this is your understanding of the information in the book. This is what we call this kind of thinking: *understanding*. Tell me what you noticed about why birds build nests.

As I guide children, I model how to record the information that we learn. It is important for children to see how good readers read information with a pen in their hand. (This is a precursor to taking notes.) I record information in the third column of the Go! Chart, labeled "Understanding."

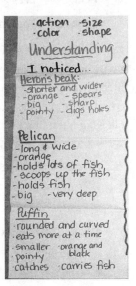

·action ·size
·color   ·shape

Understanding

I noticed...
Heron's beak:
- shorter and wider
- orange - spears
- big   - sharp
- pointy - digs holes

Pelican
- long & wide
- orange
- holds lots of fish
- scoops up the fish
- holds fish
- big - very deep

Puffin
· rounded and curved
· eats more at a time
· smaller ·orange and
· pointy   black
· catches ·carries fish

This is the anchor chart she used to record attributes of bird beaks.

The purpose of the chart is to record literal understandings. (See Chapter 3 for a detailed explanation of the Go! Chart.)

During our conversation about the text, the children and I chart facts that can be confirmed.

VICKI:	Tell me what you noticed about why birds build nests.
KYLEE:	Well, we can put that if they have their eggs all around, then predators can see them, and if they have a nest, then they can be safe.
VICKI:	You are right. If we went back into the information, where could we find that? [Returns to text]
NICKY:	It said they are protected from enemies.
GEORGE:	Yeah, but that's the same thing as predators.
VICKI:	So we could say it either way, right? It doesn't change the fact. [Charts "I noticed that birds build nests to protect the babies from predators."]
SARAH:	And they protect them.
GEORGE:	Like from rolling out of the nest.
VICKI:	Let's go back and find the nest that showed that.
GEORGE:	You know, the one in the side of the river. In the mud.

I strongly urge children to paraphrase the information because they need to learn to put the facts into their own words. Therefore, I avoid letting them read the information directly from the text to record it. As they share what they notice, this gives me a chance to find out and assess their *understanding* of the information, asking myself some of the following questions.

- Are they able to only give facts stated in the running text, or can they integrate information from the photos or other access features?

- Do they tend to want to read the information rather than putting it in their own words?

- Do they have decontextualized and descriptive language to tell about the information?

- Do their interpretations override the information? What misconceptions do they still have about the information?

- Were they able to determine importance or is their thinking still scattered about the information?

Revisit Earlier Predictions to Confirm New Information

It is valuable to return to children's predictions that they made prior to reading the text (as discussed in Chapter 4). This gives them another opportunity to work with the new information, discuss the big ideas, and confirm facts related to the new information. It also helps them to connect the new information to known information, and to clarify any misconceptions or confusion.

Guide the conversation by returning to the text and rereading as necessary to find the predicted information listed in the first column of the GO! Chart. Then alter the information on the chart as necessary so children see how their thinking changed during reading.

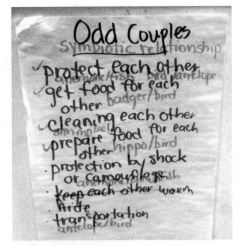

Connect the new information to earlier predictions on the anchor chart or GO! Chart.

For example, Beth was reading with her first graders about birds and what they eat. As she revisited the recorded predictions, she used the chart to visually show her children when they confirmed their thinking, how they revised their thinking for the new information, and when they still did not know whether the predicted information was correct.

BETH: Did the author tell us that some birds eat fish? He sure did. I'm going to put a smiley face beside that one. Did he tell us a bird like a pterodactyl eats fish?

STUDENTS: No.

BETH: But what else did he tell us that eats fish that we can change and show right here on the Go! Chart?

CHRIS: Flamingo.

[Beth crosses out *pterodactyl* and writes *flamingo* on the chart]

MARGO: But what about the pelican? It eats fish.

BETH: Yes, it does, but we are looking for the information in the book that the author told us. What about the next prediction: Some birds eat nuts. Was there any section that talked about birds with beaks that eat nuts? We will put a question mark beside it, because it might be true, but the author didn't tell it to us in this text.

Some teachers use sticky notes to amend earlier predictions with new information.

This activity helps students connect the new to the known. Some teachers put the new, or amended, information on sticky notes and others add the information directly to the chart. It is a visual for children to see how good readers change their thinking as they read.

Revisit Earlier Vocabulary to Develop Language

To provide another opportunity to extend and develop language, return to the vocabulary words that were introduced before the reading (see Chapter 4 for a detailed explanation about introducing these words). These words were recorded in the Vocabulary column of the GO! Chart as *predicted words* and *new vocabulary*.

Revisit the text another time to discuss the predicted words (*Which words did the author use? How did she use the word?*) and to confirm understanding of the new vocabulary words (*What does the word mean? How did the author use the word in the text?*)

Find Predicted Vocabulary Guide the conversation to have children share which predicted words they found in the text. Talk about how the words were used. Use children's predicted words as a means of talking more about the information in the text. Mark the words on the GO! Chart that were found in the text.

Children look for words that are both explicitly stated in the text or words that reflect an idea inferred in the text. Kids will often say, "The word isn't there but the *idea* is there." This is a great opportunity to show how we can use different words to mean the same thing. For example, in our second-grade discussion mentioned earlier in the chapter, the students kept using the word *predators* even though the author did not use that word.

VICKI:	We predicted the word *predators*. What word did the author use that means the same thing?
SARAH:	Enemies.
VICKI:	So we could say that birds build nests to protect the eggs from predators or from enemies, right?

I use a coding system on the GO! Chart that allows children to see our thinking about the different words. For example, a check shows words that the author explicitly used in the text (such as *straw* or *sticks*), parentheses show a word that means the same (*predators* for *enemies*), and a circle shows a word that wasn't used at all in the text but that we know applies to the information or can be inferred (*building* can be used in talking about different places that birds build nests although the author did not discuss that). Crossing out words (such as *pterodactyl*) signifies that word should not be used to talk or write about this information. (See the GO! Chart on page 93 for an example.)

The students and I continued talking through the other words they listed, returning to which birds used the different materials to build their nests. They concluded that although birds can build nests in buildings, the author did not talk about those kinds of nests.

Code	Meaning of Code	Use of Word to Retell
◆ straw ✔	◆ author word	◆ word can be used for talking and writing about the information
◆ (predators)	◆ student word, paraphrased author language, or inferred concept or word	◆ word can be used for talking and writing about the information; paraphrases information
◆ (building)	◆ concept or idea not included in text but applies to information	◆ word can be used for talking and writing about information; extends information
◆ ~~pterodactyl~~	◆ not included in text and does not apply to information or part of information being read	◆ word cannot be used to retell information, as it does not apply or is incorrect

As I cross out predicted words that do not apply to the information, I reinforce to students that they are doing the kind of thinking that good readers do: "You are learning to change your thinking as you realize that the information is different than you predicted. Good job! That is exactly what good readers do."

Clarify New Vocabulary This is the time in the lesson to confirm the new technical vocabulary, ensuring that students understand the meaning of the words and how the author used the words in context. I strive to have students share the strategies they used to figure out the meanings of the words. I teach them that nonfiction authors usually place clues for the meaning of these words right in the text (using commas, parentheses, italics, or bolded text). Good readers act as detectives to find these clues and figure out meanings.

Show children how good readers "mind the marks" as they read information. This is an important nonfiction vocabulary strategy that should become routine with reading informational text. I let students know that authors will usually "mark" a word that is important, that they want to emphasize, that might be a new technical word, or that might give the reader problems. In other words, the author has highlighted a word with *italics* or **bold font**, used parentheses ( ), placed commas before or after a word, used a larger or a **different** font, or some kind of mark that makes the word stand out. If the word is important enough for the author to "mark," then we want to take some time to make sure that we have clarified the meaning of the word. These words can be added to the Vocabulary column of the Go! Chart.

Laura Robb's (1999) *Reading Strategies That Work*, and Isabel Beck, Margaret McKeown, and Linda Kucan's (2002) *Bringing Words to Life* are excellent resources for ways to further develop vocabulary instruction.

Guiding reading of informational text for literal understanding is labor intensive in the beginning. However, the immersion, modeling, and explicit teaching will pay off. Children need to know how to read between the running text and the visuals. They need help talking about the information in the visuals. They need guidance in reading a bit, stopping a bit, thinking a bit, and talking a bit. From there, children need opportunities to try out the strategies with their own reading and to put literal understanding into their own words through writing.

Guiding Reading for Literal Understanding

→ Read only a bit of information at a time.

→ Talk about the text as you read.

→ Read back and forth between the visuals and the running text.

→ Observe and describe the information.

→ Record information.

→ Confirm and clarify predictions and vocabulary.

Teaching the Information Generation

Trying Out Evaluating Text for Literal Understanding: Ideas for Helping Students Apply the Strategy to Reading and Writing

Evaluating information for literal understanding is one of the most important—and most used—strategies that students will use for the rest of their lives, both in school and outside school. So guided practice is vital. Children need many opportunities to try out this strategy in a number of ways:

♦ In their reading of informational text

♦ In their learning logs to record information as they read

♦ In language arts to develop attribute language for the text's content

♦ In their writing of information to begin to include access features

Reading Informational Text

Provide short texts at students' instructional or independent reading levels (90–95 percent word recognition). (See Chapter 3, page 46, for more information on determining reading levels.) *Scholastic News* and *Time for Kids* are great sources of material since the articles are short, contain a variety of access features, and are published for various grade levels. Also consider nonfiction leveled books since most of them are informational texts written for K–3 reading levels.

As I mentioned, you hold guided practice sessions during language arts, science, or social studies. Start out by reading a chunk of the text aloud and encouraging students to share. From there, have students take more responsibility for the reading as it matches their developmental levels. Instruction continues in a similar manner to the instruction described in the previous section, with you

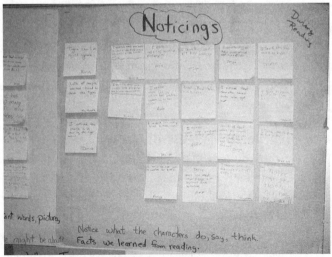

Sticky notes can be used to help students read informational text.

Reading cards help students stop and consider while reading.

initially recording the thinking on a small chart or on sticky notes. Children should not record the information themselves until you see that they are comfortable with how to read running text and access features to create literal understanding.

The following suggestions can be used in the session to guide children as they try out the strategy.

Teacher-Directed Read a Bit

Use a large index card (or half-sheet of cardstock) with an illustration of a book on one side and a light bulb icon on the other. Guide children to place the card with the book side up to mark the chunk of text that they are going to read. This marker helps them to see where to stop (at the end of the page or end of a section). This is a signal to read a bit and stop a bit. At the end of the section, guide children to turn the card over to the light bulb side (think a bit and talk a bit). The physical act of turning the card over seems to help trigger the brain to stop and talk through the text. It is also a signal for the teacher to see when each child or set of partners has completed the reading and is ready for the teacher to guide the talking and sharing part.

Teacher-Directed Talk a Bit

In the beginning it helps to guide the sharing, just as you guide the reading for children. Explain to them the kind of talk that you expect them to engage in with their partner. Talk can be focused on a photo and caption, a diagram, a chart, or other access feature. Students can use certain attributes to describe the photo. They can retell the information in their own words (from the section just read) to their neighbor. "Tell your neighbor in your own words about what we just read. Be sure to tell them some details as if they had never read the information before." This type of sharing is a precursor to learning how to share information with reports. And it is seemingly effortless and painless with bites of information and bits of sharing!

Student-Directed Read a Bit, Stop a Bit

As students become more confident and competent with how to read informational text, provide opportunities for them to buddy-read sections of information more independently. At this point, they should know to talk through the text, going back and forth between the visuals and the text. I will often give instructions or a checklist in the beginning to establish a routine.

1. Read the heading of the section and talk about it in your own words. Predict the kind of information that you might read about.

2. Choose one of the access features and talk about it with your partner. What do you notice about this feature? Listen to what your partner thinks about this access feature.

3. Buddy-read the text.

4. Go back to your feature and talk about it. What attribute words can you use to describe the feature? How does it connect to the information?

Recording Information When Reading

As children learn to read informational text more independently, give them opportunities to record information as they read. This is a precursor to taking notes. Here are some ideas for getting started.

Sticky Notes

Children can record information on sticky notes as they read. They first read a bit, stop a bit, think a bit, and talk a bit with their partner. Then they write down what they noticed in that section that they think is important. Be sure to emphasize they shouldn't copy the information but use their own words. Sticky notes can be placed on the anchor chart or Go! Chart for the teacher to guide the conversation, or used for small-group discussions.

Learning Logs

A single-column learning log labeled "I noticed . . ." or "Understanding" enables students to record information and see their thinking all in one place.

Go! Chart Format

A learning log that reflects the format of the Go! Chart works well to organize the process of reading for students. The log has three columns, labeled "Predictions," "Vocabulary," and "Understanding." Students record their predictions before reading, then revisit their predictions to confirm or adjust their thinking after reading the new information. They mark their predictions just as the teacher has modeled on the larger anchor chart or Go! Chart, to connect the new information to their predictions. As students read the information, they learn to "mind the marks" by recording words highlighted with a mark in the text. Then they talk through with their neighbor to clarify the meaning of the words.

Writing Informational Text

Students need opportunities to put their thinking into oral language so they can share it in conversations, but they also need opportunities for putting their thinking into written language. In this section I share ideas for helping students to develop attribute language (as developed earlier in the chapter) as they label and describe information.

The following teaching suggestions work best when you begin with a list of attributes related to the topic you are studying. Specifically, using an informational text that you have read and discussed with your students, brainstorm a list of attributes as a class—or extend the list created for an earlier lesson. For instance, as an extension to the lesson on bird

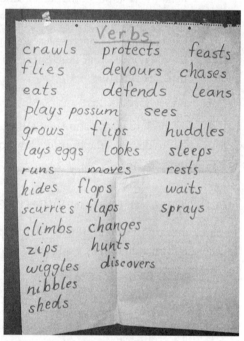

First graders used this brainstormed list of action words for writing activities about animals.

nests described earlier in the chapter, we created a list of words that describe the birds' nests using the attributes of shape (round, circular, long, skinny, fat, short, stubby, wide), materials (straw, sticks, spiderwebs, mud, leaves, moss, grass), and location (trees, branches, ground, riverbank, buildings, high, cactus). This list was used for several writing activities during the week. Children added to the list as they thought of other words.

Teaching the Information Generation

Be sure to model the suggestions below for your students. Create a text as a class before sending students off to do it on their own. It often takes several tries at shared writing before students are ready to use the strategy on their own.

Picture-Prompted Writing

Marcia Freeman (2000), an expert in children's writing, advises starting children's writing instruction with picture-prompted writing. It is also a wonderful match for extending children's observation and description skills as outlined in this chapter. Provide a picture from the text for each set of partners. Have children talk through the picture with each other using as many attributes as possible. For younger children, guide their discussion by selecting which descriptive attribute they should use: "When you describe the picture of the chameleon, be sure to use at least one of these attributes: color, size, or action. Write about the picture using one to three attribute words."

Q Is for Duck

Use the structure of *Q Is for Duck* (Folsom & Elting, 1980) to create a class attribute book. Begin with a read-aloud of the book, which asks why each letter of the alphabet is represented by the chosen word: "Q is for duck. Why? Because ducks quack."

When Sharon Becnel's first graders studied bats, they created a class book

What Do You Notice?

Describe who or what is in the picture by using at least one of the following attributes:

→ What it is doing (use a verb)

→ Where it is (the location)

→ How it moves

→ What it might feel like

→ A color word

→ A number word

→ A size word

Here is the teacher model that Sharon Becnel used.

---

using a similar format. Children chose an attribute about bats and applied it to the structure:

_____ is for bats because they _____. For example, Megan wrote, "W is for bats because they have wings." "S is for bats because they see in the dark," wrote Corbin.

Examples of children's writing from a class book

Attribute Poems

Attribute poems use patterned structures for writing that apply descriptive attributes. One of my favorites is a pyramid poem, a simple pattern that adds a new attribute to each line to build a pyramid shape. The last line adds a location attribute.

> frog
> green frog
> slimy green frog
> little slimy green frog
> little slimy green frog in the pond.

Beth used a simple but powerful patterned structure in her classroom with her first graders. When studying weather, her students decided which type of weather to write about and three attributes. Then they used this pattern:

- subject
- attribute

- ◆ attribute
- ◆ attribute
- ◆ subject

Andrew wrote:

storm
windy storm
crashing through the air
raining like crazy
storm

Example of a child's attribute poem

Using Access Features in Writing

Professional writers of informational text need to make choices about the kinds of access features they will include so that their readers will understand their topic to its fullest. So, as students begin to write informational text themselves, make them aware that they have similar choices to make. They can put the information into prose, but how else can they show or represent it? How can they organize the information into chunks that make sense for the reader?

Throughout the course of the school year, create opportunities for your students to put information into words and visuals. As you create class books or conduct shared writing, help students see how to organize the information with headings, illustrations, lists, and other access features. Provide guided practice in including access features in writing.

As her first graders made class books about their Thanksgiving feast, Beth modeled the decisions authors make. Specifically, she showed how to organize the information with a table of contents. For other projects, she included an index in their books on farms, a glossary in their books about robins, and diagrams in their books about ladybugs. Through these shared writing experiences, her students began thinking how they could organize and share information using access features. By the end of the year, they made decisions about the kinds of features they would include in their reports. They saw themselves as information literate, using information accurately and creatively.

Laurie Castagna's second-grade students did research and wrote reports about jungle animals. As they planned how to share the information, they made decisions about how they would organize the information and how they would use access features to evaluate the information at a literal level. Laurie had worked with them throughout the year,

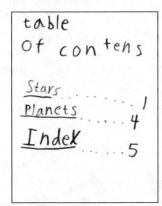

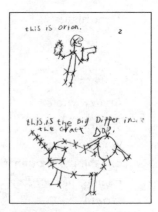

Joseph used access features in his report and included illustrations and captions.

giving them many opportunities to learn about and create these features. Students had to include a photo and caption, bold print, a diagram about their animal, a table of contents, a glossary, and an index.

Below are suggestions that teachers have used to help primary-grade students learn how to use access features in their own informational writing. Again, be sure to model each of these ideas before students try them out on their own.

Consider Organization in Shared Writing

As you make class books, include ways to organize the information for the reader. Use headings, tables of contents, or indexes. Talk through how to help the reader find the information they might need.

A class book's table of contents

Write Captions for Pictures

Copy a page from an informational text containing a photo and caption. Cover the caption with white correction tape or a sticky note. Have students look at the photo, read the surrounding text, and write a caption for the photo, based on what they learn. Teach students that *the caption should show the connection between the photo and the information.* Ask, "Why is the visual on this page?" "How does it help the reader learn about the information?"

Teaching the Information Generation

Write Headings

Many times nonfiction books for young readers do not have headings. After talking through a two-page spread, have children come up with a heading: "How can we tell the reader what this section is about?" Place white correction tape across the top of the page and write a heading through shared writing or interactive writing.

First-grade example of a diagram in a class book

Create Diagrams

Move students beyond "drawing a picture" to labeling a diagram. As young children draw pictures of animals, teach them how to label the parts and create a diagram.

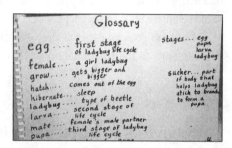

Student-generated glossary

Create a Class Glossary

Choose several vocabulary words and work with children to define them in their own words. "How can we tell this to a neighbor who doesn't know what this is?"

Assessing Evaluating Text for Literal Understanding: Behaviors to Look for in Student Reading and Writing

As children are learning to evaluate text for literal understanding, we need to keep an eye on their progress so we know how to support them and plan instruction. You can do that in a number of ways: observe and listen to the conversations, use checklists, assign learning logs, and use content-specific assessments.

Observe and Listen to Conversations

While I was visiting Mandeville Elementary, Arlene Gieg tracked me down in the hallway to share how her second graders were using access features to find information they needed. During independent reading, one of her boys had discovered in his nonfiction book a photo of a penguin, with the caption, "The jackass penguin, a flightless seabird, is found nowhere in the world except off the coast of southern Africa." As you might imagine, like so many second graders, he thought the bird's name was hilarious and wanted to share it with the other boys.

The buzz started as the other boys grabbed other nonfiction books and began their search for the jackass penguin. "Where should we look first?" "Maybe look at other pictures and see if you read another caption like that." "Should we use the table of contents to find another jackass?" "No, no! That would take too long." "I know, I know! Use the index. Look it up under *jackass*." "Or try penguins and see if they list the kinds of penguins." As Arlene observed, she realized that this was learning in action. These boys had learned how to find the information they needed. They knew it would take too long to read the entire text, so they let the access features guide them.

Listen to your students as they work in pairs and small groups. Watch them as they begin to read an informational book. Do they know how to find the information that they

Behaviors to Look and Listen For

(Behaviors that indicate students are reading informational text to create literal understanding)

➜ Beginning with heading before they read or look at the visuals

➜ Reading back and forth between visuals and text (take note of where they begin)

➜ Describing the photos and visual features using attribute language

➜ Including information from the visual feature when talking through the text

➜ Inferring the connection of the visual to the text

➜ Sharing the information in their own words

➜ Paying attention to captions in order to figure out the connection of the text to the photo

➜ Knowing where to look to find information "in the neighborhood of" (table of contents) or the "exact address" (index)

need using the access features? Are they beginning with the headings and the visuals as they read? Do they move between the text and the features? Are they able to talk with a partner about what they notice? Are they making connections between the visuals and the text? Do they only read the visuals and not the text? Do they read straight through the text without reading in "bits" to stop and talk? Observation allows you to see student behaviors and hear their thinking to know if they are learning how to access information to evaluate it at a literal level.

Use Checklists

Self-generated checklists provide a written record of observations. To create one, start by determining the learning behaviors upon which you will focus. The list on page 108 is a good beginning point. Think: *What do I want to see my students doing while reading information?* These behaviors should be modeled extensively, and students should be trying them out for themselves.

I find it helpful to assess only three to five behaviors at a time. These can be general behaviors for reading information (such as beginning with the heading or reading in bits) or more specific behaviors (such as how to use a table of contents or how to use captions effectively). When assessing, have children read in pairs or small groups.

Checklists are also valuable to the students themselves. Give partners a checklist with the same three to five behaviors that you will assess on your checklist. Be sure to write the checklist in child-friendly language to help them focus their discussion. Then, when it is time to assess, students will be aware of your expectations.

Assign Learning Logs

Learning logs require students to put learning into writing, and they will give you insight into their understanding and ability to record that understanding. As you assess these logs, ask the following:

- Do students include important information in the Understanding column or just write any facts?

- Are they including information from photos and other access features?

- Can they put information into their own words or do they copy from the text?

- Do they revisit their predictions, noting the changes in thinking and new information?

- Are they noting words that have "marks" in the text to clarify?

Practice Content Assessment

The more children learn how to read informational text, the more they understand content at a deeper level. As you assess understanding of the strategy of evaluating for literal understanding, make sure you also assess understanding of content. After all, that is the purpose of the strategy. Each of the above assessments assesses the strategy in relation to the content.

You can do that not only by observing students and using checklists, but also by questioning them or asking them for retellings. Retelling is a powerful form of assessment because it provides a window into student thinking and language. To administer a retelling, give individual students a preselected piece of informational text at his or her instructional level. Then ask the student to read it either aloud or silently and then tell the information in his or her own words. As students retell, allow them to use a photo or visual feature as a springboard (Cambourne & Brown, 1987). Choose only a chunk or bit of information. Ask children to retell as much as they can from the text: "How would you tell this to someone who has not seen this photo (or map, diagram, chart, etc.) or read this text?"

In listening to a student retell, you will be able to know if she has effectively accessed the information (used the access features to get the information), evaluated the information (connected the facts and the photos at a literal level), and understood the information (the content itself). You should not assess memory, but understanding. Was she able to use her own language to retell the information? Did she include information from the visuals? Is she becoming information literate?

Have students pair up and retell the information to each other. One partner can retell one section of the text and the other can retell the next. Use a checklist to guide conversation and assess understanding.

In time (after many, many opportunities for oral retellings), children can write their retellings—not written reports, but short retellings of "chunks" of information. In the process, children will write about what they know, an important skill for effective writing (Calkins, 1994; Graves, 1994; Suid & Lincoln, 1988). Can they put their understanding of the information into writing? I have found that the more opportunities children have to write retellings, the more fluent their writing becomes.

Closing Thoughts

Evaluating text for literal understanding helps young readers to know how to focus their energies during reading. It helps them to access the new information and then gives them a tool for evaluating the information at a literal level to get the facts. Students learn to read informational text by connecting the information in the text to information in the visuals and other access features. Learning to label and describe information lays the groundwork for students to be able to build a more critical understanding of the information. They have moved one more step toward becoming proficient readers and information-literate students—with confidence, eagerness, and enthusiasm.

CHAPTER 6

Evaluating Text
for Critical Understanding

"I think I know why alligators hide in water. I bet it's because they can sneak up on other fish and animals." Second grader Tony was thinking with the other students in his inclusion classroom about the book *Hiding in Plain Sight* (Fehlner, 1999), which describes a variety of animals and their camouflaging attributes. Today the students were evaluating that information by making interpretations about it and connecting it to things that they knew. Devon added, "I hide under my bed in a black shirt from my brother—and he can't find me. So I could hide in plain sight." Meagan later wrote, "Snakes hide in wagons. They curl up like a Frisbee."

As their teacher, Cathey Graves, listened to their conversation and then read the children's writing, she got a glimpse into their thinking. Cathey knows that for students to become information literate, reading the facts is not enough. It is the beginning point. They must evaluate the information critically. Students must interpret facts and connect them to their lives "to evaluate information critically and competently" (*Information Literacy Standards for Student Learning*, 1998). (See Chapter 1 for an explanation of the information literacy standards.)

This chapter focuses on the cognitive strategy of evaluating text for critical understanding. As students learn how to interact with the text and the author at sophisticated levels, they develop a personal, more critical understanding of the information. They will then be able to "use the information accurately and creatively" (Standard Three), because they have a deeper understanding of the content and can share that understanding with others.

The Strategy of Evaluating Text for Critical Understanding: An Overview

Critically evaluating text is more than learning facts, describing facts, or bridging the new to the known. It is working with the new information to *fully integrate* it into the known—to make sure it fits and to know where it fits in the cognitive backpack. It requires readers to draw conclusions, to infer and interpret the information, to work with the information until it makes sense (Elder & Paul, 2003). Without this kind of processing, learning is limited to memorization of facts.

Like assembling a jigsaw puzzle, evaluating text critically takes time, patience, pondering, and reasoning. Proficient readers know that some puzzle pieces are usually in the text and that others are in their prior knowledge. They consider the facts and what they already know about the topic, working with the pieces until the puzzle is complete by engaging in inner conversations as they evaluate the information critically.

Basic readers, however, have not yet developed these skills because they are so focused on the facts as they read. They do not or cannot relate new information to prior knowledge (Pressley & Woloshyn, 1995). Or when they do, their connections are random and scattered. Most basic readers do not know how to talk through their thinking; instead, they restate or rephrase facts (Glaser, 1989). They need guidance to find the right connections and to use those connections to build knowledge. They need help in developing their inner voice and having inner conversations.

There are three kinds of thinking that readers can use to evaluate text critically: *literal-level thinking* (identifying, labeling, describing the information), *interpretive thinking* (analyzing, evaluating, responding to the information), and *comparative thinking* (comparing prior knowledge and experiences to new information) (Elder & Paul, 2003; Hansen, 1981; Pressley & Woloshyn, 1995; Pressley et al., 1992; Rosenblatt, 1994; Tierney & Pearson, 1992). Chapter 5 focused on literal-level thinking, which is an essential starting point for critical thinking. This chapter extends the ideas from Chapter 5 by focusing on interpretive thinking and comparative thinking, which help children to draw conclusions about information. As children learn strategies for developing these forms of thinking, they learn to evaluate information critically.

A Mind Picture for Evaluating Text for Critical Understanding

In one of my favorite episodes of *The Bill Cosby Show*, Bill is home watching the kids while his wife, Claire, is away on a trip. He is confronted with making breakfast for the troops, and so he takes the easy way out and serves them leftover chocolate cake. His kids, of course, love it. They start chanting, "Dad is great! He gives us chocolate cake!" And they continue chanting all day long until Claire arrives home later and discovers the sneak sweet treat.

When I share this story in the classroom, the kids also love it! I ask them, "Which would you rather have for breakfast, cereal or chocolate cake?" And their usual answer is a resounding "chocolate cake!" Then I tell them this is a mind picture we can use to know if we are reading information critically.

I start by explaining that cereal thinking represents literal-level thinking. I ask them to consider their favorite cereal with marshmallows. When poured into a bowl, it is very easy to pick out the marshmallows from the cereal (as most kids do!). No matter how much you stir the bowl of cereal, you can still separate the marshmallows from the cereal. This is like basic readers' thinking as they read information—the facts stay separate from their thinking. No matter how much you try to stir it up—no matter how many times they read the same passage or how many questions you ask—the facts remain separate and static. These readers do not yet know how to combine the information with their prior knowledge to draw conclusions.

Proficient readers, on the other hand, mix their thinking with the facts to create critical understanding, much the way bakers mix ingredients together to create a chocolate cake. They cannot pull out the cocoa and the sugar once the cake batter has been mixed, which is fine because no one wants to the taste ingredients separately (even cocoa by itself is bitter!). We want to taste the flavor of all the ingredients mixed together. Chocolate-cake thinking is mixing literal understanding (the facts) with interpretive thinking and comparative thinking. The more the reader mixes these ingredients together, the more they form the batter of understanding, so to speak. The more opportunities the reader has to work with the new information, the deeper his understanding of the information.

Children need to know how to distinguish *facts,* which are universal and don't change from person to person, from their *thinking, feelings,* and *experiences* about the facts, which are unique. I refer to the GO! Chart (see page 115) to show that these strategies are important ingredients in chocolate-cake thinking:

- Facts are *understanding* the information (literal thinking): These are the facts that will be found in the informational text.

- My thinking or feelings are *interpretations* about the information (interpretive thinking): These are drawn from the information in the text as well as from personal experiences; although unique to the individual reader, conclusions must be accurate for the content.

* My experiences mean *connections* to the information (comparative thinking): Experiences are unique to each reader. There are self experiences, other-text experiences, and world-knowledge experiences (Harvey & Goudvis, 2000; Keene & Zimmerman, 1997).

Predictions	Vocabulary	Understanding	Interpretations	Connections	Organizing

The GO! Chart can help develop "chocolate-cake thinking"

In the following sections you will learn how to help students engage in "chocolate-cake thinking" to develop inner conversations as a means to evaluate information for critical understanding.

Teaching Evaluating Text for Critical Understanding: A Way to Introduce and Develop the Strategy

In this section I suggest ways to show children how to interpret new information and connect it to their lives and prior knowledge, so that they gain a deeper, richer understanding of that information. I refer to the teaching tools introduced in Chapter 3:

* Tools for making thinking explicit: think-alouds, modeling, and explanations

* Tools for organizing and recording thinking: anchor charts, GO! Charts, sticky notes, and learning logs

* Tools for talk: group conversations and pair and share

Over the course of several weeks, conduct *critical conversations* as you read an informational text with your students. As you think and talk about the information, record student interpretations and connections on the GO! Chart.

Explicitly Teaching Interpretation

Interpretive thinking is the glue that holds the facts together and builds critical thinking. However, it is often difficult for children to engage in interpretive thinking (Pressley & El-Dinary, 1992). Teaching children to ask interpretive questions when they read can help.

Asking Interpretive Questions

I was once talking to a group of second graders about scientists, when one little boy, George, observed, "The more questions a scientist asks, the smarter he gets." And he is right on target. Chris Tovani (2000), author of *I Read It, but I Don't Get It*, believes that it is difficult to interpret without first wondering. In fact, she contends that it is unreasonable of teachers to expect students to make interpretations before they question. "Inferential thinking is born out of questions the reader has about information stated directly in the text" (p. 87).

We can learn from George's observation. The more questions readers ask—questions that stem from what the readers notice about the text—the smarter they get. Good readers are a bit like scientists this way—they ask questions and then try to figure out the answers.

Teach children to ask "scientist" questions based on information they find in the text. Then, as they try to answer the questions, push them to consider the information in light of what they know and what other information the text contains. It's three easy steps to more critical thinking, more engaging conversations, and deeper understanding of the information!

Get the Facts: Observe and Describe To introduce interpretations to a group of second graders using Diane Noonan's *Bird Beaks* (1994), I carried out the following think-aloud. I wanted students to know that interpretations start with the information.

VICKI: Today when we read about bird beaks, we want to observe their size, their shape, their color, and their actions. Remember that these are called attributes. Today we are going to think about these attributes as we read. We are going to use the *thinking skills of a good scientist and a good reader.*

When teaching interpretation, start by reading an informational text and listing facts and/or attributes in the "Understanding" column of a GO! Chart (as described in detail in Chapter 5). I read one page of the book about bird beaks and then began our critical conversation at the literal level by looking for the facts.

Teaching the Information Generation

VICKI:	What do you notice about these birds that live by the sea? The author shows us two birds and gives information about their beaks. Remember, we are observing what their beak does (the action), the color, the size, and the shape. [Reads:] "Some birds that live by the sea have long, thin beaks. The birds poke their beaks into the sand, looking for shellfish and sea worms."
MARISSA:	It has a long, long beak.
VICKI:	What do you notice about the beaks for these birds that live by the sea?
GEORGE:	It's pointy.
JAMAL:	It's black.
VICKI:	What is the bird doing?
SARAH:	Reaching for food.
STEVE:	Eating.
MIKAL:	Poking.

After establishing literal-level understanding about the information in the text, guide the discussion toward framing scientist questions about the information.

Understanding	Interpretations
The seabird's beaks are_____. ♦ long ♦ pointy ♦ sharp ♦ used to dig holes ♦ used to reach food	I wonder why . . . how?

Facts from the text are listed in the first column.

Ask "Scientist" Questions About the Facts: Why, How, When, and Where

After getting the facts, it is time to push students to think beyond them by turning them into interpretive questions, or "scientist" questions: *why, how, when,* or *where*. Here's how I might introduce this concept to students:

VICKI:	There are four questions that scientists ask that help them to find out about the world. And good readers ask those same questions to think

about what they are reading and learning.

The first two are the most important questions that we are going to ask today: WHY and HOW. For WHY, we might look at our facts and ask, Why is it that shape? Why is it that size? We are going to think about the attributes that we observe about the beaks and ask a WHY question.

Another "scientist" question is HOW? How does the bird catch food? How does it peck at a tree? As we think about the attributes we are going to ask a HOW question.

Those are the most important questions and the ones we ask first. But we can add two more to our list: WHERE and WHEN. Where does the bird find food? Where does it live? When does it use its beak?

Moving children from facts to interpretations of those facts helps to focus the interpretative conversation and anchor children's thinking. When guiding the conversation, I show children how we can take a fact, or an attribute, and think about it with WHY: *Why is this true?* For instance, in this second-grade conversation we looked at the shape, size, and color of the bird's beak and asked: *Why is it this shape, this size, this color?*

Michael Pressley found that turning a fact into a WHY question pushes the learner to think about the fact, activate prior knowledge about the fact, and answer the question by filling in knowledge gaps about the fact. His research on asking WHY questions about the facts, using a technique he calls Elaborative Interrogation, shows the technique increases memory and comprehension (Pressley & Woloshyn, 1995; Pressley et al., 1992).

Reader reads:	Reader thinks:
♦ Pennies cost more than one cent to make.	♦ Why does it cost more than one cent to make a penny?
♦ Trees and other woody plants don't grow in the flooded, low-lying marshes of Florida.	♦ Why don't trees and other woody plants grow in the marshes?
♦ Insects are found almost everywhere on the planet except in the ocean's salty waters.	♦ Why don't insects live in salty water?
♦ Manatees and dugongs are endangered animals.	♦ Why are manatees and dugongs endangered?

Michael Pressley's technique, Elaborative Interrogation, asks readers to turn a fact into a WHY question: *Why is that fact true?*

Teaching the Information Generation

HOW is another interpretive question that extends thinking: *How can the bird use this beak to get food? How does the beak's shape help it? How does the size of the beak help?* I have found WHY and HOW to be higher-level questions that usually require more critical thinking to answer. Literal-level questions usually include *what, who, when,* or *where. What color is the bird's beak?* (black) *What does the bird eat?* (shellfish and seaworms) *Where does it look for food?* (by the sea) All answers are explicitly stated in the text. On the other hand, *why* and *how* usually require information that must be interpreted, calling on prior knowledge and experiences or looking between facts for answers.

WHEN and WHERE are alternative questions for interpreting, as they sometimes push readers to fill in the blanks with thinking. *Where might the heron find this kind of food? When might it use its beak besides when it's looking for food?*

In the beginning, you should model asking and answering interpretive questions for students to give them a sense of what the process looks like. You should also guide the conversation toward important key concepts (as will be discussed in the following section). Have children frame their questions with the wondering phrase, "I wonder why . . ." or "I wonder how . . ." Children soon learn to anticipate the interpretive questions of WHY and HOW and will begin asking their own questions.

VICKI: Today we are going to use our noticings to think more about these birds. Thinking about the birds that live by the sea and what their beaks are like—let's read our Understanding list again of attributes: long, pointy, sharp, used to dig holes, used to reach food.

Here are the first two questions for us to think about: I wonder WHY their beaks are long, sharp, and pointy? HOW do you think these birds get their food with their beak?

Answer the Questions and Prove Your Answers Readers need to do more than ask questions to gain deeper understanding and better comprehension of the information they read; they need to *answer* those questions.

VICKI: Scientists ask WHY, HOW, WHERE, and WHEN questions. But then they try to answer those questions and make sure they can prove their answers. And how will we prove our answers? From the facts the author shared in the text or from what we know or experienced—our connections. This book doesn't tell us everything about bird beaks, does it? And so you can prove your answer by thinking about what you already know. We can prove it from the book or from our head.

The Benefits of Seeking Answers to Interpretive Questions

➜ Develops an attitude of wondering and inquiry

➜ Activates prior knowledge and integrates information at a deeper level

➜ Focuses reading on important information rather than random facts

➜ Helps monitor comprehension, as students know when they didn't understand what they read

➜ Increases memory and comprehension

➜ Creates more accurate inferences

This is where the reasoning takes place for the beginning of critical understanding. Interestingly enough, it is the attempt—not necessarily the correct answer—that helps to increase comprehension and memory of the fact (Pressley & Woloshyn, 1995; Pressley et al., 1992). The energy it takes to tap into our prior knowledge makes the information more meaningful and therefore more memorable. As young readers learn to ask WHY and HOW questions, they think about the information and tap prior knowledge to answer the questions.

As students look for possible answers, encourage them to frame their responses around the term "I think . . ." This emphasizes that these kinds of answers usually require interpretations, as readers must consider the clues in the text and their own connections to come up with information not explicitly stated.

VICKI: Here are the first two questions for us to think about: HOW do you think these birds get their food? WHY do you think their beak is long, sharp, and pointy?

KYLEE: It's sharp, so I think the food probably gets hooked onto the end.

NICKY: It pokes it with the beak.

VICKI: So you are thinking that it gets hooked onto the end as they poke the food? Create that picture in your mind. Can you see the bird poking its food and it sticking on the beak?

GEORGE: It can make sure it's food.

VICKI: What do you mean by that, George? So you think . . . what? Can you tell us more?

GEORGE: That it's not a rock or something.

MIKAL: Like if it can eat it?

GEORGE: Yeah, so it can poke it and know if it's a fish or a rock.

VICKI: So George is thinking it might use its beak to get its food but also to make sure it can eat what it finds.

Understanding	Interpretations
The seabirds beaks are_____. ◆ long ◆ pointy ◆ sharp ◆ used to dig holes ◆ used to reach food	I think . . . . . . it's sharp for food to get hooked to the end. . . . it pokes its food with the beak to get it. . . . it makes sure it is real food by poking it. . . . it might cut with its beak.

As children offer their thinking, encourage them to dig even deeper by asking questions such as *Did you find clues in the text? Did part of the answer come from your head? How did you know that? What made you think that?*

Finding Answers to Interpretive Questions

➔ Reread only the parts of the text that you need to find the answer (use the index, photos, captions, or skim the section).

➔ Find facts in the text.

➔ Think about what you already know about the topic.

➔ Create a picture in your head to help you.

➔ Use the clues and your prior knowledge or experiences to try to answer the question.

➔ Share your thinking about your answer.

➔ Prove your answer!

During this conversation, record all interpretations that are valid in the column labeled "Interpretations." By valid, I mean they must be based on solid facts. So be aware of misconceptions. Weigh children's thinking. Consider the following transcript of second graders working through their interpretations about the heron's beak. My job as teacher was to weigh their thinking and guide them toward shared understanding.

NICKY: I think maybe [the heron] could cut with it.

VICKI: What makes you think that, Nicky?

NICKY: It's long and pointy and sharp like scissors.

VICKI: So you are thinking that because it looks like scissors it might also be used like scissors?

JEROME: Maybe instead of, like, food, it could work on paper and cut out.

VICKI: Now I have to ask, Jerome, what makes you think a bird would want to cut paper? We have to think about that.

MARISSA: Maybe it could cut for a nest.

GEORGE: Or to break stuff.

VICKI: So could we say we think that maybe it uses its beak for more than eating?

MARISSA: For making a nest.

GEORGE: For cutting up its food.

This teacher is recording interpretations as "I think . . ." on a GO! Chart.

When children do the mental work to try to answer the why and how, the information they are learning is integrated into long-term memory—and discussions are engaging and lively! Children begin to talk about ideas rather than just facts.

When teaching this strategy, be sure to break down the text into small chunks (as discussed in Chapter 4), and discuss and record the facts for one chunk at a time. Then move on

Teaching the Information Generation

to making interpretations. Move back and forth between the Understanding column and the Interpretations column—from the facts to thinking about the facts. Continue reading the text in the same manner: read a section, record facts, then interpret the facts in that section. For instance, in *Bird Beaks* we read about only one type of bird at a time, recording its attributes. Then I moved from the Understanding column to the Interpretation column for each bird.

Focusing on the Key Concepts

Children need help putting the puzzle together. They need to see the big picture, or the whole puzzle, so to speak. As you guide conversations, focus attention on the larger ideas or concepts rather than getting bogged down in facts. This is a critical skill for all readers. For example, in the lesson about bird nests discussed in the last chapter, one of the big questions the author of *Eggs and Baby Birds* (Shirley, 1993) asked was, "Why do birds build nests?" However, the information in the running text in the section we read was on the materials birds use:

"Some birds build their nests on the ground. This nest was built by a mallee fowl. It is a huge mound of soil, leaves, and small sticks."

"This is a song thrush at its nest. The nest is made of dried grass, and it is lined with mud."

"A hummingbird's nest is tiny. This long-tailed hermit hummingbird's nest is made of cobwebs and moss."

Focusing on the facts would most likely lead to literal understanding. But putting facts with thinking to figure out the WHY and HOW should lead to critical understanding and help students draw conclusions about the information.

It was my job as the teacher to guide the conversation back to the big concept of why birds build nests—to help students interpret the facts. For example, I chose interpretive questions that would guide students to consider why the mallee fowl might build its nest on the ground. The children made interpretations from the facts.

Vicki:	Where is the nest?
Tyler:	On the ground.
Jamal:	That large pile.
Nicky:	Underground.
Vicki:	You can't see the eggs, can you? Why do you think the mallee fowl built her nest like that? [*interpretive question*]

TYLER:	Where you can't see them.
SARAH:	Maybe they are way down inside there.
TYLER:	To keep them away from predators.
GEORGE:	Plus you wouldn't notice it.
TYLER:	It's camouflaged.
VICKI:	Because what do we know about why birds build nests? [*key concept*]
NICKY:	To protect.
TYLER:	So predators don't come.
GEORGE:	So predators don't eat them.
KYLEE:	So people can't find them.
VICKI:	So we are thinking the mallee fowl built her nest on the ground to protect her eggs. [*conclusion*]

On each page, I used the interpretive questions to get children to consider why the bird used the kinds of materials it did, why it built the nest where it did, and how its methods and materials helped to protect the eggs and baby bird. These second graders didn't only describe what was in the photo or the text, but thought about the nest in light of why the bird might build a nest like it did, making interpretations based on information in the text and their prior knowledge.

VICKI:	We read one section today in our book about eggs and baby birds. Let's go back to the beginning of the section and see if we can answer the big question the author was asking: Why do birds build nests?

I did not want students to memorize all the individual bird names and the exact details of each bird's nest. After reading, thinking, pondering, and talking, they should be able to understand the key concepts (why birds build nests) and to share examples to demonstrate their understanding.

Interpretive conversations lead to drawing conclusions. These types of conversations help young readers determine the author's intent and purpose. At the end of our discussion on bird beaks, Angela shared, "I think that each bird's beak matches the kind of food it eats!" That's chocolate-cake thinking in action.

Teaching the Information Generation

Prompt	Behavior	Benefits to Students
"I wonder . . ."	♦ student chooses fact (or attribute) and asks wondering question ♦ considers why the fact is true	♦ activates prior knowledge ♦ creates sense of inquiry ♦ piques interest
"I think . . ."	♦ student tries to answer question, looking for clues in text ♦ uses prior knowledge and experiences to fill in gaps ♦ posits an inference or interpretation	♦ activates prior knowledge ♦ elaborates to fill in gaps ♦ fits information into content domain ♦ integrates information ♦ creates visual for new information
"I feel . . ."	♦ student gives opinion about information ♦ supports opinion with details/facts from text or experiences	♦ activates prior knowledge ♦ involves affective domain ♦ creates personal interest

Explicitly Teaching Connections

Connections help readers better understand new information. Ed Vockell (1995) contends that as the reader connects new information to familiar information, the connection serves as an "informal but effective advanced organizer" to make cognitive links to the new information—to help the reader find where the new pieces of the puzzle fit.

The quality of the connection counts, however. Research confirms that the type of connection readers make impacts the outcome of the learning (Zook & Maier, 1994). The connection must be "rich enough" to help the learner construct a solid understanding of the new information—it must show the reader where to make the cognitive link to better understand the new information. For example, in Cathey's second-grade class, Devon, a proficient reader, connected playing hide-and-seek to his class's science topic of camouflage. As he visualized himself under the bed in a black shirt, he better understood the concept of being absorbed into the background because the color of his shirt was the same color as the night (chocolate-cake thinking).

Basic readers, on the other hand, often make connections that do not help them understand the new information, as their connections are more peripheral to the information (cereal thinking). For instance, Jackie said that the alligator in the lake "hiding in plain sight" reminded her of her grandfather going fishing. She could not relate the connection back to the information. She picked up on the lake and then connected that to her grandfather fishing in a lake. She ended up thinking about her grandfather fishing rather than what it means to camouflage and hide in plain sight. Her connection did not help her to better understand the topic.

I have found that children need explicit instruction, guidance, and support to make effective and meaningful connections that lead to new understanding of the information. This means doing more than asking general questions like *What does this remind you of?* It means showing them how to engage in comparative thinking. They need to hear expert readers model rich connections, and they need to see how connections are grounded in facts. They need to develop comparative thinking.

Developing Comparative Thinking

When beginning instruction in comparative thinking, encourage children to compare their concrete experiences to the information they're reading. Then gradually move them toward making more interpretive connections. Eventually, with guided practice, children will be able to do this on their own. The following sections show you how to get them there by showing them how to:

- Create concrete connections
- Make parallel connections
- Compare and contrast attributes

Create Concrete Connections Introduce connections by showing children how to compare a concrete experience in their world to information in the text. Have children think about the fact in light of what they have seen, heard, felt, tasted, touched. How have they used their senses to experience the concept they are reading about? What experiences have they had that prove this?

Begin with a fact from the text (or listed on the GO! Chart), such as "Birds build nests in trees" or "The moon seems to change shape," and ask: "How did you know that?" or "What experience have you had that proves or supports that fact? Have you seen this for real?" Once you've got the children thinking, go on to say something like:

Teaching the Information Generation

Good readers think about facts as they read facts. They think, Where have I seen this? Have I tasted this? Heard this? Felt it? Experienced it? Maybe I read about this somewhere or watched something about it on TV. They think about what experiences they have had with that fact.

Choose a sensory-rich topic that is familiar to young children, such as family, money, the moon or sun, stars, food, or animals. Chocolate was a good topic for creating concrete connections with Beth's group of first graders.

BETH: We wrote on our chart the fact that chocolate melts. We read it in our book, but I bet some of you already knew that. How did you know? Or what evidence do you have that proves that?

NICK: Because if you don't eat it fast enough in the summer it will melt.

BETH: Has that ever happened to you?

SEAN: Once I had a candy bar and it melted in my hand.

ALE: Yeah. When it's in the sun a long time it melts.

BETH: You know that because you had it melt in your hand, huh? Or maybe you have been in the sun and seen it melt. You have *experienced* it.

JOSEPH: Whenever you have chocolate in your hand it melts and the chocolate drips.

SASHA: It makes a mess.

BETH: When good readers read facts from a book, they think about where they have experienced that idea. And when you think about the time that chocolate melted in your hand, or when you were in the sun, or the mess that it made when it dripped, you can get a picture in your mind. That helps you to understand and remember the fact that chocolate melts.

As her students compared fact to experience, Beth made each connection explicit. She focused the connections to specific facts about chocolate. The experience needed to support the fact: *How is your experience like the information? How do they connect?*

BETH: Here is the fact: Bakers use chocolate to make cakes, pies, and cookies. What evidence do you have? How do you know it's true?

JENNA: My mom bakes and uses stuff like that.

BETH:	Will that work? How does that connect to our fact?
MARGO:	Her mom did it.
KYLE:	It's your family.
BETH:	Could my evidence be: My dad uses chocolate over his ice cream.
ZOE:	No.
BETH:	What makes you say that?
SEAN:	You can use chocolate on your ice cream.
BETH:	But does that go with bakers making cookies? Our fact?
ZOE:	Because it's baking and it's cookies. That's nothing about baking.
VICTOR:	But what about chocolate pie? I eat chocolate pie.
BETH:	So pie is a good connection to help us see our fact in our head. But ice cream won't work because it doesn't go with the fact about baking.

Children need to share their thinking aloud to become aware of their inner conversations. In so doing, it allows you to see where and how they need to be guided to read informational text more critically. As her students shared their thinking, Beth was able to uncover their inner conversations and, in the process, misconceptions about the information.

BETH:	Here's our next fact: When you eat chocolate, it gives you energy. How do you know that?
CHRIS:	I know that when my dog eats chocolate he has to eat grass.
BETH:	Is that because dogs get sick when they eat chocolate? Does that support the fact that chocolate gives you energy? Let's make sure we know what energy is.
CHRIS:	It's a stomachache.
BETH:	Can someone share with Chris what energy is?
MARGO:	It makes you want to exercise.
KYLE:	It makes you have muscles.
BETH:	Does it make you sick?
CLASS:	No.

Teaching the Information Generation

BETH:	Can we use a dog getting sick to connect to chocolate giving us energy? If not, what else can we use?
LIZZIE:	One time my mom baked a chocolate cake, and when I ate a piece I jumped up from the table and ran all around.
MATT:	My mom says I'm crazy when I eat too much chocolate.
BETH:	So, Chris, do Lizzie's and Matt's experiences help you to better understand about chocolate giving us energy?

During the conversation, it is important to show students that our connections help us to understand information. Take the connections back to the fact. Show students how their experiences help them to create a mind picture about the fact.

To motivate children to share, start with "I know because. . . ." This allows children to see that their experiences support the fact, and that when we think of our experiences, it helps us to feel more knowledgeable about the fact. You can list the fact and then chart student responses. For example:

I know that spiders make different kinds of webs because . . .

♦ Jamie saw a long spiderweb on the playground.

♦ Larissa saw a weird-shaped web.

♦ Karina saw a TV show about spiders making webs.

♦ Jerod saw a spider making a web on the water.

The connection must relate directly to the content. Otherwise, it is a peripheral connection and does not have the potential for deeper learning. For example, these kindergarten students had to relate their experiences about spiders to the specific information about *spiders making different kinds of webs*. Not any connection about spiders would do.

As you guide the conversation, chart student responses on the GO! Chart in the Connections column. This allows children to see how you are grounding connections to the information listed in the

This teacher is helping a child make connections back to information on the GO! Chart.

Understanding column (as described earlier in the chapter and in more detail in Chapter 5). This also allows you to show children explicitly how to use their connections to better understand the information.

Make Parallel Connections "Chocolate is like ice cream because it melts," Zachary said during Beth's class discussion. Zachary did not share a direct experience with chocolate melting, as others did. Instead, he shared a parallel connection: *What experience have I had with something that is similar?*

Many children have experiences in their everyday world that parallel attributes of the phenomena being studied, or *parallel connections.* Proficient readers use parallel connections to compare the information in the text to something familiar in their world. By looking at the similarities between what they know and what they don't know, they can learn more about what they don't yet know. Andie Cunningham (Cunningham & Shagoury, 2005) finds this type of learning powerful in working with her kindergartners. In *Starting with Comprehension,* she shares how metaphors help us to understand abstract concepts. They make the abstract more concrete. Learning through parallel connections is learning through metaphor.

To help children learn to make parallel connections, revisit the facts recorded earlier in the Understanding column on the GO! Chart. Guide students to compare one or two attributes to something in their own lives and talk about those comparisons.

Here I guided the critical conversation about bird beaks with the second graders to create parallel connections.

VICKI:	We are going to think how each of these birds does things like us. We might not have seen a heron before, but we can think what we do that reminds us of how the heron uses its beak.
	First, let's make sure we know how the heron uses its beak. Look at our list of attributes. What does it look like? What does it do with its beak?

Understanding
The seabirds beaks are_____.
◆ long
◆ pointy
◆ sharp
◆ used to dig holes
◆ used to reach food

I focused student attention on the action attribute—how the bird uses its beak. At the same time, we considered the size and shape of the beak. We began to compare those attributes to similar items and actions in our experiences.

VICKI: Let's think. What do we do that is similar to how a heron gets its food?

TYLER: Like a knife.

VICKI: How is a heron's beak like a knife?

TYLER: It's long and sharp.

JOSE: And he stabs his food.

VICKI: So we can say the heron stabs like a knife. What else can you think of that we pick food up with by stabbing?

SARAH: A fork.

VICKI: How is a fork like a heron's beak?

SARAH: You stab meat and stuff with a fork.

JOSE: It's long and skinny like a fork.

VICKI: So we can say the heron's beak is like a fork. So that when I think of the heron's beak, I can picture in my head a fork and how I use it to stab meat.

Encourage children to make comparisons by using the word *like*. What does this look like to you? What do you know that is like that? Guide the conversation and chart children's responses, always directing their connections back to the information. "How does this help us create a mental picture of the information? How does it help us to know about the information that we are reading?" From there, guide children's thinking back to the attribute and make sure they know how the attributes are similar.

VICKI: So what shape is the beak for stabbing food?

JEROME: Long and pointy.

VICKI: What else can you think of that we use for stabbing that is like a heron's beak?

MIKAL: Like a butter knife.

VICKI: Now let's think about that. How is a butter knife like a heron's beak?

Creating Parallel Connections

➡ Choose two to three attributes to compare.

➡ Guide connecting conversation.

➡ Brainstorm experiences similar to the attribute.

➡ Emphasize the word *like*.

➡ Take connections back to the information.

MIKAL:	I don't know.
VICKI:	Then let's think how they look alike or if they look different.
SARAH:	Different. It's not pointy.
VICKI:	What do you do with a butter knife?
GEORGE:	Spread stuff.
VICKI:	So you don't use a butter knife for stabbing?
SARAH:	It's not pointy!
VICKI:	So Mikal, would that help us to think about how a heron's beak is like a butter knife? We're thinking about sticking food to pick it up.

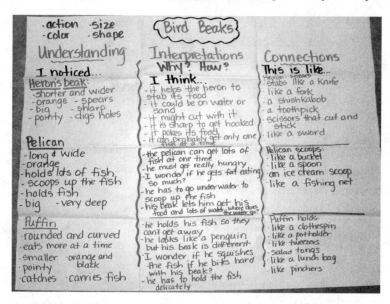

This GO! Chart reflects the parallel connections second graders made with Vicki.

In the beginning, you may have to suggest parallel connections for children to consider. For instance, when talking about how the pelican scoops fish into its beak, I made a connection to things we use to scoop. I asked, "What do fishermen use sometimes to catch lots of fish at once?" Through our discussion we talked about a fishing net and how it is similar to a pelican's beak. Then the students suggested a shovel, an ice-cream scoop, and a bucket for scooping. The brainstorming began! By the end of the conversation, they had a mental image of what the pelican's beak looks like and how it's used to gather food.

Teaching the Information Generation

I usually try to find several parallel connections to an attribute so that children have several opportunities to work with the new information. It gives them different chances to make connections and create visuals for the information. In so doing, they are creating anchor points for the information, and the more anchor points a reader has to connect to, the more meaningful the new information (McPherson, 2000; Pressley & Woloshyn, 1995; Pressley et al., 1992).

Compare and Contrast Attributes Sometimes children's connections "miss the mark" because they do not have enough prior knowledge or experiences to understand the common attributes, or they have a limited understanding of the attributes. So teach students to go a bit further and to *contrast* as well as compare attributes.

"My parents are like dictators," Celia shared as we studied democracy in third-grade social studies. I wanted to make sure Celia had a clear understanding of the concept of dictatorship, since her connection made me think that her understanding was a bit wobbly. We needed to first identify what Celia thought was similar about her parents and a dictator: "How are your parents like a dictator?" We revisited the information in the text about a dictatorship. Then the class helped her compare and contrast her parents to dictators.

"Well, my parents boss me around and dictators boss people around," she said. Comparing and contrasting the attribute of telling people what to do allowed us to analyze and dig a bit deeper. We went back to our interpretive questions: Why do parents tell children what to do? Why do dictators tell people what to do? We talked through our interpretations, returning to the social studies text and our own experiences. Celia was able to grasp how her parents were different from dictators, and in the end she had a concept about dictatorship that she originally missed.

These discussions are lively, engaging, and rich in understanding. As children talk, help them weigh out their connections and integrate the new information into their prior knowledge effectively and accurately.

Modeling Rich Connections

Children need to make connections that are "rich enough" to help them learn the new information, as discussed earlier. They need to hear and see rich connections. Authors use such connections all the time. For example, I use Martin Jenkins's (1999) book about emperor penguins, *The Emperor's Egg*, to demonstrate this. I read sections out loud to the children, identify facts about penguins, and point out Jenkin's parallel connections to those facts. Here's an example. Jenkins writes:

"What's more, there's nothing for the father penguin to eat on land. And because he's egg-sitting, he can't go off to sea to feed. So that means two whole months with an egg on your feet and no dinner! Or breakfast, or lunch, or snacks. I don't know about you, but I'd be very, very miserable."

In this instance, he compares one attribute of the father penguin to his own life. Jenkins considers the emperor penguin going without food for two months to his own life of eating three meals a day. By thinking about this comparison, he interprets how miserable waiting so long between meals must be.

Another good example can be found in *Bird Beaks* (1994). Diana Noonan begins her book with this connection:

"Some people use a knife and fork to eat their meals.
Others use a spoon or chopsticks.
But birds use their beaks.
Each bird has a special beak to catch its favorite food."

I guided the conversation with interpretive questions: "Why do you think the author talks about a knife, a fork, a spoon, and chopsticks in a book about bird beaks? How does this help us to think about birds and how they eat with their beaks?"

VICKI: I think Diana Noonan was letting us listen to her inner conversation as she was thinking about bird beaks. It sounds like bird beaks made her think of how we use knives, forks, spoons, and chopsticks. The author compared how we eat to how a bird eats. What do we use to eat?

SASHA: You eat with a spoon.

KYLE: A fork.

VICKI: What else did she say?

CHRIS: Chopsticks.

VICKI: So not everybody eats with the same thing, right?

GABBY: It depends on what you eat.

VICKI: Great job! That's exactly what the author wanted you to think about. How is a bird eating like us eating?

GEORGE: A spoon has a little thing in it for soup and a beak has a little thing in it to hold fish.

MARGO: Like chopsticks for Chinese food.

ZOE: So that might mean it picks up little stuff too. So maybe birds pick up little things as well.

VICKI: So you are thinking that maybe some birds have thin beaks like chopsticks. The author's connection got us thinking about the information that we will read.

Noonan provides us with a familiar connection, which helps us, as readers, get ready to learn about bird beaks. Her connection showed the reader where to begin making cognitive links to the new information. As we read about each beak, we picture in our minds how we eat with different instruments for different kinds of food.

To model rich connections in books, find and read informational texts in which authors share concrete and parallel connections to the information. Look for metaphors, similes, and analogies. Make the author's connection explicit to students and then talk through how it relates to information in the text. Help children to see how the author's connections help the reader to visualize and better understand the new information.

Favorite Books for Rich Connections

Animals in Hiding, Melvin Berger, Newbridge

Bird Beaks, Diana Noonan, Wright Group

Chameleons Are Cool, Martin Jenkins, Candlewick Press

Dinosaur Cousins, Bernard Most, Harcourt Brace

How Big Were the Dinosaurs? Bernard Most, Harcourt Brace

How Do You Lift a Lion? Robert E. Wells, Albert Whitman & Company

Is a Blue Whale the Biggest Thing There Is? Robert E. Wells, Albert Whitman & Company

The Emperor's Egg, Martin Jenkins, Candlewick Press

The Wetlands, Marcia Freeman, Newbridge

What's Smaller Than a Pygmy Shrew? Robert E. Wells, Albert Whitman & Company

Grounding Connections in Facts

Children must come to understand that *their connection must be grounded in the fact.* To reinforce this point, I bring two to three helium-filled balloons to class and tell the children, "These balloons are like our connections. They can help us learn about the information that we are reading."

Picture the children's excitement. Then imagine their disappointment, and even shock, as I let one of the balloons go and watch it float up and away. Helium balloons have to be anchored to keep from floating away. Likewise, if a child makes several connections as she's reading, she might be excited. But unless those connections are anchored in the text, the thinking floats away from the information—sometimes far, far away! And basic readers get lost in the connection rather than using the connection to learn the information.

In this way, connections can be a pitfall for basic readers. They can be counter-productive, or lead to misconceptions, if left unaddressed. For example, while discussing how the mother bird protects her eggs, Hank's thinking wandered as we talked about the kingfisher.

VICKI:	But look at the picture again of the kingfisher. Where is this nest?
TYRONE:	In the mud.
MILO:	On the side of the river.
SARAH:	There's the hole. I can see it.
JEROME:	Where are the eggs?
KYLEE:	She is protecting the hole.
TAQUITA:	That's so nobody can get them.
HANK:	I have a connection! Once I saw an egg on the ground and it was squished and there was a baby bird in it.

If left on his own, Hank would continue to focus on his own experience rather than the information in the text. So I helped him tie his experience to the facts in the text and use his connections to learn about the book's big idea.

VICKI:	Hank, let's make sure that our thinking isn't just floating away. We need to tie it to the information. So let's think back to the eggs that you saw and think how they are like or different from the eggs we are reading about.

KYLEE:	Different.
VICKI:	How were they different than these other eggs in the book?
BRIANNA:	Those eggs weren't in a nest.
VICKI:	And what happened to the eggs that you saw, Hank?
HANK:	They got squished.
VICKI:	How do you think the eggs that Hank saw might help us to think about why birds build nests?
GEORGE:	If they had been in a nest, they wouldn't have got squished.
KYLEE:	And they could be born.
VICKI:	So, Hank, what is one reason why birds build nests?
HANK:	To make 'em safe.
VICKI:	So when you think about birds building nests, you can picture in your head those squished eggs and you will remember that birds build nests to protect their babies, right?

It is important to let children know when their thinking is floating away. For instance, as I was reading about manatees in one of the classes, third grader Mariah shared her connection of how she saw a manatee on her vacation to Florida. Josiah then connected to her connection by talking about his vacation to Disneyworld. The class then wanted to talk about having fun at Disneyworld and not manatees! This conversation should not be about Disneyworld, but about seeing a manatee in person and thinking how this connection can help us to visualize the fact that a manatee weighs 3,600 pounds. Children need to learn how to take their connections back to the information.

Evaluating information for critical understanding requires comparative thinking. Proficient readers compare what they already know to the new information, using the lens of the familiar to try to make sense of the new information.

To wrap up the connecting conversation, allow children to express their thinking and feelings as opinions—to judge the information. After discussing spiders with second graders, I asked them, "So tell me, what do you think?" Antoine remarked, "This is cool that spiders suck the guts out of their prey. Yeah, man!" Analeise countered, "That's the grossest stuff I ever read." "Hey, spiders live on a web and so do we—on the computer! Get it?" laughed Nicky. When children respond like this, it shows that they are learning to evaluate information critically because they are using inner conversations.

Trying Out Evaluating Text for Critical Understanding: Ideas for Helping Students Apply the Strategy to Reading and Writing

Children have wonderful thoughts about the world around them—and when we help them explore those thoughts, their ability to think critically grows. As I pointed out in the last section, conversations are an excellent way to do that, but they're not enough. We must also give students hands-on reading and writing activities. The ideas in this section are intended to guide you in helping children interpret and find connections to the information they are learning so that when they write about the information, they "use information accurately and creatively" (Standard Three; see Chapter 1).

Trying Out Interpretations

After discussing Martin Jenkins's *Chameleons Are Cool* (2001), Beth decided to have her students write their interpretations. "We have all these facts that we recorded about chameleons. Now we are going to make our interpretations and support them with facts. I want you to think if chameleons would make good pets or not. Tell what you think and why." To prepare them to write, she had her students share their interpretations in pairs.

As Beth walked around her room, she heard Isaac say that chameleons would make good pets because they eat insects and would therefore get rid of annoying mosquitoes. Victor said he thought they wouldn't be good pets because they are grumpy.

However, Isaac challenged him: "What facts make you think they are grumpy?"

"His face makes him look grumpy. The way his mouth turns down," Victor replied.

Chloe thought a chameleon would be a good pet because they are quiet. "If you are doing your homework, then it won't bother you." Her partner, Nicholas, however, disagreed. "They won't make noise and have fun with you," he countered. Beth listened to make sure students were tying their thinking to the facts. The buzz in the room told her they were.

After their sharing, Beth had her students use index cards to organize their thinking for writing. On the front side of the card, each student wrote either "I think chameleons would make good pets" or "I think chameleons would *not* make good pets." On the back, they wrote three facts about chameleons that supported their opinion. Beth was leading these first graders into writing persuasive text by encouraging them to share their beliefs and back them up with facts. Based on information from their cards, each student wrote a page. The finished pages were collected into a class book, which became a favorite addition to the class library. Because they were given this opportunity to try out interpreting through reading, writing, and sharing, these first graders soon made the strategy their own. The following ideas help students try out interpretations.

Comparing and Sharing Interpretations

Pair children and let them share and compare their interpretations. Let them talk through their thinking with their partner. By doing so, they will discover and strengthen their inner voices and critical thinking. Most children need the modeling before they can share, so it's probably best to carry out this exercise after a whole-group discussion and the GO! Chart recordings.

Have partners choose a fact and ask a "scientist" question (or interpretive question, as discussed earlier in the chapter) of their partner. Then ask partners to work together to answer the question, looking in the text and using their prior knowledge. Encourage students to first try out a WHY or HOW question as they talk through the information. Have them use the phrases "I think . . ." and "I feel . . ." when providing interpretive answers. For example, after reading about and discussing bird beaks, I had these second graders form pairs and share their interpretations.

Students talk through interpretations.

VICKI: I want you to turn to a partner. You have observed all these facts about the puffin's beak that we recorded. Now I want you to choose a fact and ask your partner one of the scientist questions. Ask them a WHY question about the beak, or a HOW question. *Why is the beak that shape? How are they going to eat?*

Then you only have one minute to see if you can answer it! Don't forget to talk about what you noticed in the picture, what you read, and what you already know to answer the question.

Students learn to find facts, then ask scientist questions and try to answer those questions. After multiple opportunities to ask and answer interpretive questions, students can begin to share their interpretations, as Beth's first graders did in the anecdote at the start of the section. In this case, students share their interpretation (thinking or feeling) first about the content. They frame their sharing with "I think. . . ." Then they support their interpretation with the facts from the text. For example, second grader Jacob shared,

"I think jumping spiders are awesome!" His sharing partner, Marissa, asked for his facts. He went on to add that he thought they were awesome because they were found on Mt. Everest. "It would be so awesome to be 22,000 feet up off the ground!" Marissa shared that she thought it must be hard to be a tarantula because they lay millions of eggs. "I wouldn't want that many babies because it would be too hard to take care of them all." (The following section provides more suggestions that can be incorporated into a share and compare as well.)

Interpreting Photos

Tap the power of the picture. Give copies of photos from the text to pairs or small groups of children. Use the phrases "I noticed in the picture" and "I think in my head" to get the children interpreting. Model how *I noticed* requires details that you can see in the photo. "I noticed the chameleon is catching a bug." *I think* requires interpretation of those details. "I think the chameleon is hungry." Have children talk about what they notice and what they think from the photos.

After children have had several opportunities to interpret photos using these phrases, move them into writing by using a frame like this: I think _____ because I noticed _____. "I think it must be lunchtime because I noticed the chameleon is eating." "I think the chameleon is happy because he just got to eat." "I think the bug is unlucky because the chameleon ate him."

This picture from Joy Cowley's *Chameleon, Chameleon* (2005) is used to help students interpret text.

Two-Sided Writing

Two-sided writing is the application of Beth's idea above for organizing student thinking and writing. I have used, and extended, this idea many times and found it to be a powerful tool for teachers to show children how to integrate voice into their writing of information.

Children begin by writing an opinion or interpretation on the front side of an index card. You can provide a general statement/question that children must support or not (as Beth did above, "Are chameleons good pets?"), or the students can write their own opinion or interpretation (as Jacob shared above, "Spiders are awesome!"). Then they turn the card over and on the back side list two to three facts that support their interpretation. Students complete three to four cards before writing. Tell children that when we write information, we write from both sides of the card—we use "two-sided writing," which is chocolate-cake thinking.

I think . . .	Facts to support my thinking

On their two-sided writing cards, Beth's students wrote about chameleons as pets.

> I think chameleons are not good pets because their eyes always follow me. Their eyes can move back and forth at the same time. They are rude because they stick their tongues out. If you stuff a cricket in their mouths, they will bite you. That is why chameleons are bad pets.
> Matthew

> I think chameleons make good pets. Chameleons are interesting because they can do a lot of things. Chameleons' eyes are not spooky to me because they are cool. Chameleons are slow. Chameleons are quiet. Quietness is good for me because I can do my math. I have enough money to buy one. So, there you have it. If chameleons aren't good pets, I don't know what is.
> Chloe

To help children think more critically as they write information, try this variation. On the front side of the card, children record one to three facts about the information. I point out to children that this is their inner conversation they are sharing and it shows chocolate-cake thinking!

Some children need a visual to distinguish facts from interpretations and connections. Simply add the icon of a book to the fact side of the card, and a light bulb to the thinking side. Children learn to draw the icons themselves on the card, and think: *Did this come from the book or from my head?*

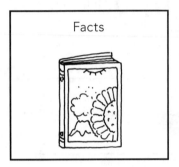

Erin Castagna used a variation of this idea and had her second graders create flip books for trying out interpretations. Students recorded facts about the coral reef on the front of each flap. Then they wrote their interpretation on the bottom flap under the fact.

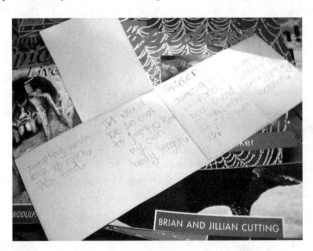

This is an example of Erin's flip-book idea.

Teaching the Information Generation

The flip books served as an organizer (and reminder) that when they wrote, they should write information on both sides—top and bottom. Annie wrote:

Coral Reef

I love the coral reef. It is beautiful like my mommy. It has many colors like pink, blue, and purple. It looks like a beautiful underwater garden. I think it probably looks like a garden because of all these colors. The coral reefs are like fish because they come in all sizes and shapes. Did you know that polyps grow onto the coral reefs to get bigger? That would be cool if polyps made our houses, too. Coral reefs are in danger from waves and hurricanes. Not only can hurricanes destroy our houses, but they affect the coral reef and all the fish that live there, too!

Although Christian also wrote about the coral reef, you can hear in his writing how he evaluated the information with his interpretations:

Coral Reef

Do you think about where you are going the next day? Are you busy? Do you have to wake up early? Well if you went to the coral reef, you would have a busy day. The fish are always swimming and the reefs are always growing. A coral reef looks like a beautiful underwater garden. It must be full of many colors. Coral reefs are created by millions of tiny animals called coral polyps. If I were a polyp, I wouldn't like being attached to animals my whole life! The largest reef is the Great Barrier Reef. I would love to go fishing here so I could get lots of fish to eat! A coral reef is home to many sponges, shrimps, crabs, and other small animals. Do you think a lot of the other animals get eaten by other animals in the reef?

In his book *Reality Checks*, Tony Stead (2005) says that children's personal experiences and opinions have a place in nonfiction writing. However, he also provides the caveat that they should not dominate the writing and that their thinking must be related to the facts. The index cards and flip books seem to help children keep that in focus. As well, because children share and compare their interpretations orally before writing, their writings

Here are pages from the class book entitled *Chameleons Are Good Pets.*

develop more fluency and children are more engaged in their writing. (And I find reading all those passionate informational writings so much more enjoyable!)

Trying Out Connections

Making connections is easy for most students. Making rich connections is not. For example, Nate wrote: "Hurricanes, waves, and waste threaten the reef. When we had a hurricane, I had to evacuate." His connection did not reflect critical understanding of the information. The following ideas are intended to help students like Nate make richer, more meaningful connections.

Scouting Comparisons in Books

As discussed earlier in the chapter, it is important to model how authors use connections in their writing. So have students become scouts for comparisons as they read informational texts in the content areas during literacy instruction, independent reading, at the library, and at home. For example, after Cathey discussed with her students how the author used comparisons in *Hiding in Plain Sight* (Fehlner, 1999), ("This lazy alligator looks like a log"; "The spots on this butterfly's wings look like an owl's eyes"), she had them scout for parallel connections in other sources, such as trade books and magazine articles. The students were amazed at how many other comparisons, often voiced as similes, they found!

Have students bring in these texts when they find comparisons and share. Chart the different ways that authors compare to use as models for children. You will soon hear, "Here's another comparison! The swamp is like a giant sponge." "I found a good connection. The gecko looks like a brown, dried-up leaf."

Marcia Freeman's (2000) *Non-fiction Writing Strategies* is an excellent source of ideas for developing comparisons, as well as other ideas for informational writing.

Comparing Attributes in Writing

Following the reading of an informational text, have children create comparisons using attributes from the text or recorded on the GO! Chart. Guide children by asking them to compare one attribute from the information to their own connection: action, size, shape, texture, color, location. "What is similar about this attribute to what you know?" For younger children use a frame sentence to guide the thinking and writing: A _____ looks like a _____ (or feels like, moves like, is shaped like, etc.). For example, in a kindergarten class, I used the text *Chameleon, Chameleon* (Cowley, 2005) with the frame: A chameleon looks like _____. The kindergartners used the photos and their own connections to complete their writing frames.

> One chameleon looks like my bedspread.
>
> The big chameleon looks like a striped blanket.
>
> The tiny chameleon looks like a leaf.
>
> That chameleon looks like a lizard my brother caught.

To extend this writing activity, have students add the fact that shows the connection. A _____ looks like_____ because _____. In another class, a first grader pointed out once that "the chameleon looks like Mrs. Castagna's shirt because they are both green and blue."

For older children you might ask, "What does this look like to you?" (or feel like to you? move like to you? seem like to you? etc.), using one of the specific attributes. As children become more accustomed to describing attributes, they can be asked to identify an attribute and then compare it to something they know.

Model for students how to use comparisons as similes and metaphors: *The chameleon walks slowly like a sloth. Walking like a tightrope walker, the chameleon creeps along the branch. Like a giant to a frog, the chameleon is much larger in size. The yellow frog is as tiny as a Matchbox car. Some chameleons are as big as a squirrel and others as tiny as a matchstick.* Similes and metaphors are comparative connections that help children to connect what they know to the new information.

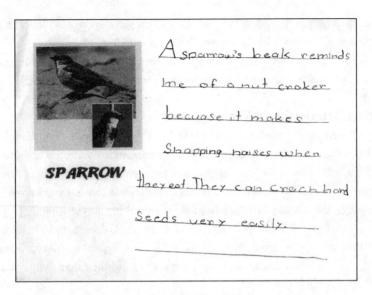

A sparrow's beak reminds me of a nut craker becuase it makes snapping noises when they eat. They can crack hard seeds very easily.

SPARROW

Here is a student writing sample featuring connections.

Combining Interpretations and Connections in Writing

As proficient writers compose, integrating unfamiliar information with prior knowledge and experiences, they create new levels of understanding. This should be our goal for children. Whether they're writing about bird beaks, coral reefs, or chocolate, we should give them the tools they need to write with critical understanding. Here are two ideas to help you do just that.

Putting the "Most" Into Their Writing

Bernard Most's trade books about dinosaurs are a great model for writing with interpretations and connections. In *How Big Were the Dinosaurs?* (1995) and *Dinosaur Cousins* (1990), he incorporates connections, facts, and interpretations. In *How Big Were the Dinosaurs?* he compares the attribute of size.

Read the book and talk through the format with children.

1. First he gives a parallel connection to one of the dinosaurs, comparing its size to something that we know. ("Shantungosaurus was so big, it was about 50 ducks long.")

2. Then he gives a fact about the dinosaur. ("It was one of the biggest duck-billed dinosaurs ever found.")

Teaching the Information Generation

3. Last, he gives an interpretation or asks his own wondering question about the dinosaur ("I bet it could make the loudest quack ever!")

Use a similar format for children's writing. Choose an attribute from the Understanding column of the GO! Chart to use for comparing.

1. Make a comparison using *like*.

2. State a fact or attribute.

3. Tell what you think.

A _____ is like _____. (parallel connection)
It _____. (fact or attribute)
I think _____. (interpretation)

The heron's beak is like a fork.
It stabs its food.
I think it must be cool to always have a fork
ready to eat!

Creating Voice

The activities I present here provide opportunities for children to bring voice to their writing—to share their inner conversations. After multiple opportunities with guided practice, strong voice will begin to emerge in children's informational writing. In *Reality Checks*, Tony Stead (2005) asks children to consider, "What words can I use to make my information sound really interesting?" Weaving their interpretations and connections into their writing is one way to do that. Second grader Michael wrote about the Titanic.

The Titanic sailed April 10, 1912. On the fourth
day it saw a big giant ice burg. It started slowing
down but got fast again. So it stopped 3 miles away
from it. How come it did not stop? I think I know!
I think the propellers were too small. The front
went down first, then the ship flooded. It split. The
back came up. It stood straight up for 5 minutes.
It went under. That's sad, isn't it?

As children try out the strategy of evaluating information critically, they offer their thinking and their language about what is being studied. They put their own unique stamp on the learning. In *The Art of Teaching Writing*, Lucy Calkins (1994) reminds us that understanding is not about just a collection of facts, ". . . it's about the author's relationship to those facts and about the meaning an author builds from and around those facts" (p. 446). Victor thought the chameleon looked grumpy, Marissa thought it would be tough to be a tarantula, Annie thought the coral reef was beautiful like her mom, and Michael thought the Titanic sank because of design flaws. Through their interpretations and connections, these information-literate students built critical understanding "from and around" facts.

Assessing Evaluating Text for Critical Understanding: Behaviors to Look for in Student Reading and Writing

Engaging interpretive and comparative thinking not only helps students understand informational text, but it also helps teachers assess that understanding. As Beth, Cathey, and Erin read their students' writings, they could assess what each student understood about the science content and the process of making interpretations and connections. Their insights enabled each teacher to adjust and redirect her teaching over the following weeks. In this section, I discuss ways to help you assess your students' critical understanding through observing student behaviors in their conversations, reading, and writing.

From Michael's writing (on page 147), we can assess not only his understanding of the concept, but how he evaluated the information critically. Specifically, we can tell Michael did the following:

+ Accessed the information efficiently and effectively. He gathered informational facts about the Titanic that pertained to its sinking.

+ Evaluated the information critically and competently, thinking through why the Titanic might have sunk. He offers his thinking, as well as his emotional response, to the information.

+ Used the information accurately and creatively. He was able to share information and his inner conversation about the Titanic. He wrote from a place of critical understanding.

Michael is on his way to becoming an information-literate second grader.

By reading her students' writing closely, Cathey gained insight into their understanding about the concept of hiding in plain sight and their process for reaching

Ability to make interpretations and connections:
Is the child able to provide a connection or interpretation? Does she at least attempt to interpret or connect the information to what she already knows, or does she only rephrase or restate information?

Quality of interpretation or connection:
Is the child able to relate his thinking back to the information? Can the child relate the facts or attributes to personal experience? Is the connection random or, at most, peripheral to the author's point?

Understanding of the new information:
What is the child's understanding of the information? Is she able to use her experiences or thinking to better understand the information, or does she have misconceptions about the information?

that understanding. She also had a brainstorm, which she noted in her journal: "Perhaps the answer to the question of how we, as teachers, need to help our students become information literate for the twenty-first century might very well be hiding in plain sight!"

As you teach the strategies of making interpretations and connections, listen to student responses during class discussions. Read closely written responses in student learning logs and writing assignments. As you assess student responses, consider the following:

- The student's ability to make interpretations or connections
- The quality of the interpretation or connection
- The student's understanding of the new information

The table on page 150 and the questions above will help you look for behaviors to determine if students created a literal understanding, a struggling critical understanding, or a strengthening critical understanding about the new information. (Also, see appendix, page 217, for the Retelling Information Rubric.)

As Cathey observed her students' conversations and writing, she realized that:

- Tony interpreted the information as he thought about why alligators would hide in plain sight in the water for all to see: "I bet it's because they can sneak up on other fish and animals." This let Cathey know he was thinking beyond the facts

Evaluating Information Critically With Connections

Ability to Make Interpretations or Connections	Quality of Interpretation or Connection	Understanding of New Information	
Student restates or rephrases information.	No attempt to make a connection; student cannot move beyond text; cannot access prior knowledge or experiences about new information	Memorizes or copies information	**Literal Understanding:** *No mental interactions between thinking and facts*
Student provides connection to information or interpretation about information.	Random or peripheral connection; thinking not grounded in facts; beginning attempts at making connections	Cannot take thinking back to information; student separates thinking from facts or has misconceptions about information	**Struggling Critical Understanding:** *Student is able to move between facts and thinking, but not yet able to use thinking to create understanding*
Student provides connection to information or interpretation about information.	Relates thinking back to information: supports interpretation with facts; can identify attributes of information and relate to personal experience	Uses experience, connection, or thinking to understand content better; student can talk about content using connections or interpretations	**Strengthening Critical Understanding:** *Student able to move between facts and thinking to create understanding of information*

on the page, connecting them to what he knows as he tried to figure out *why*. She identified his critical understanding as strengthening.

♦ Jennifer was still literal in her thinking because she only copied a fact directly from the text. She was unable to apply interpreting or connecting. Cathey knew the best she could expect from Jennifer at this point was memorizing facts.

♦ Cathey could see that Devon understood the concept, as he used his personal experience of hiding under the bed in a black shirt. He also was able to make a connection that was meaningful and rich. His connection helped him to picture the science concept and strengthen his understanding.

♦ John's response was interpretive, but showed that he missed the concept. He wrote, "I think it would be cool to be an alligator because you can eat people." Cathey would need to encourage John to interact with the information more, using his thinking to interpret the information. She knew his concept of animal camouflage was weak.

♦ Meagan's connection of how the snake curled up like a Frisbee when hiding in a wagon reflected her strengthening critical understanding of the concept. However, it also surprised Cathey. It revealed more than just her knowledge of the concept. "This is a child who usually shuts down when asked to write or even pick up a pencil. I was utterly amazed at what she did. She exhibited more language ability than she has ever shown before! Her illustration was beautifully done and showed a bird's-eye view of the snake curled up in the wagon, hiding in plain sight."

By assessing these three areas (i.e., students' ability to make interpretations and connections, the quality of those interpretations and connections, and students' understanding of new information) you can plan and differentiate instruction more wisely.

The chart on pages 152–154 suggests ways to adjust your teaching as you observe and assess your students. The first column lists different types of *learning behaviors* when making connections. The second column describes the *cognitive response* that behavior reflects as the student creates literal or critical understanding. The third column suggests an *instructional response* that will help bridge the student's connections to the information they are learning for deeper understanding of the content.

Learning Behavior	Cognitive Response	Instructional Response
No attempt to connect "Frogs hide in plain sight." [copied directly from text]	Student is staying in the text; no interaction between thinking and text, or no thinking about the text.	Provide modeling and guidance in how to make connections; use closed (teacher-directed) connections.
Connection not anchored "This reminds me of when my cousins play hide-and-seek and we have fun at their house. I like going to my cousin's house."	Student is beginning to move beyond the text or facts and interact with thinking; student is not sure how to activate connections or find "entry point" to connect new information to prior experiences or knowledge; needs guidance in finding the correct domain/ category in schema to attach new information.	Think aloud to model how to anchor connections to new information; use of visuals is critical for activating connections; use closed connections and help student to develop language to connect information to experience.
Anchored connection "I know why alligators hide in water in plain sight, so they can sneak up on other fish and animals."	Student is able to show the relationship between his connection to prior knowledge or experiences and the new information in the text	Encourage student to explain how his connection relates to the new information and how the connection helped him to better understand the new information.
Literal connection "This reminds me of the time I saw a frog hiding on a green leaf."	Student has some experience with or prior knowledge of concept; information is connected at the literal level; found correct domain/ category; reader visualizes information or concept due to prior experience.	Reinforce how the connection is anchored to the information and how the connection helps the reader to visualize the information; guide student to consider comparing attributes with closed connection conversations.

Teaching the Information Generation

Learning Behavior	Cognitive Response	Instructional Response
Parallel connection "Snakes hide in a wagon. They curl up like a Frisbee." "I hide under my bed in a black shirt. I hide in plain sight."	Student finds a connection that allows him to compare and contrast a parallel experience, thus allowing him to interact between prior knowledge and the new information; increases understanding of the concept by thinking about the common attributes; sees commonalities and differences in the known and the new; provides figurative language for talking/sharing about the information.	Encourage use of parallel connections in writing about the information; provide opportunities for students to share their connections and thinking with others.
Missed connection "It reminds me of my grandpa because they are like him. They go fishing."	Student makes connection to the wrong domain/ category or reflects that he did not understand the new information.	Reexplain and guide the student toward a connection that will help him to understand the information.
Closed connection Teacher: "How are things sometimes in plain sight and we don't see them? Let's make a list of things that are the same color as their background."	Student follows teacher's prompt with "closed" connections; teacher provides "entry point" for connection, helping student to find the domain/category in which to integrate the new information.	Choose one attribute and brainstorm comparisons; shift responsibility to open connections throughout year; provide opportunities for student to share anchored connections in writing.

continued

Learning Behavior	Cognitive Response	Instructional Response
Open connection "This reminds me of chameleons that change colors. Only they change when they are mad, and these animals change to hide."	Student finds the domain/category and integrates the new information; reader knows how to interact with the text and make appropriate connections to prior knowledge and experiences	Praise students for finding effective connections; help them to see how their unique connection helps to create their understanding; encourage use of open connections in writing about the information; provide opportunities for students to share their connections and thinking with others.

Adjusting teaching for stronger connections and deeper understanding.

Closing Thoughts

If we expect our students to evaluate text critically we must explicitly show them what that looks and sounds like. We need to teach them how to have conversations in which they exchange ideas about information rather than just restating information. And we need to do this often enough that they have inner conversations as they work with the author and interact with the text.

Stephanie Harvey and Anne Goudvis (*Strategies That Work*, 2000) contend that interacting personally with text allows the reader to "see a new perspective, or form a new line of thinking to achieve insight" (p. 143). When we provide these critical-thinking opportunities, we create a context for "ah-ha's." As students learn how to make interpretations and connections, they constantly amaze me. Who would have thought that a snake would hide in plain sight curled up like a Frisbee?

Teaching the Information Generation

CHAPTER 7

Evaluating Text for Conceptual Understanding

Brandi Appe was reading *From Egg to Robin* (Canizares & Chessen, 1998) with her kindergartners. At the end of the reading, Brandi asked, "Let's look at the facts in this book. Does the order the author put them in matter?" A discussion broke out about the bird, the nest, and the egg. "Well, first the robin has to lay the egg before the egg can hatch," said one student. "Yeah, but even before that she has to build the nest," said another.

Brandi confirmed their thinking. "So it sounds like you are saying that order matters. If order matters, then what kind of organizer should we use?"

Raphael jumped in. "I know. Use the sequence map, because order matters!"

Rebecca countered, "But the robin will grow up and build another nest and lay another egg and it will hatch and it will go on and on. So it's a circle." Brandi took her cue from Rebecca and led these kindergartners in creating a cyclical map to show the life cycle of the robin.

Debbie Sterling's second-grade class was reading a short text about Jane Goodall and her work with chimps. After the reading, Debbie asked her students to think about how the author organized the information. "Did the order of the information matter in this book? Think about the facts and talk with the people around you. Then we will figure out the best way to map out the information." After a bit of discussion, students shared their thinking. One group came up with the idea of using a concept map. They shared their reasoning: "If you put Jane Goodall in the center of the map, then you can list around her name all the things that she did."

However, Maddy, a student in another group, disagreed. "Like order doesn't matter! She can't become an adult before she becomes a baby. Order matters. We have to show that." This group decided to use a sequential map to show how the author described her life from childhood to adulthood.

These primary students are becoming information literate. They are talking through the text at an abstract level. They are thinking beyond a list of isolated facts. They are thinking about how facts are related within a text. These students are learning how to think conceptually.

When students think conceptually, they seek out relationships and patterns among those specifics—or facts. Conceptual understanding occurs when students have successfully organized those facts into categories to create meaning.

The last chapter considered how to help young readers evaluate text for critical understanding as they made connections to prior knowledge and experiences. This chapter looks at ways to help students develop conceptual understanding.

The Strategy of Evaluating Text for Conceptual Understanding: An Overview

Teaching children to think conceptually is more critical now than ever before. However, this is easier said than done because most of us are more comfortable teaching facts than how those facts fit together. It's worth the effort, though. And it's essential.

Think about these expectations outlined by NAEP (*Reading Framework for the 2003 National Assessment of Educational Progress*, 2003). Students must:

♦ Consider the text as a whole, forming a general understanding of the information

♦ Focus on specific parts of the text, linking information across the text

♦ Think beyond the text, connecting the information to prior knowledge and experiences

♦ Consider why and how the text was developed, evaluating the content and organization of the text

To meet these expectations, students must be able to think conceptually— specifically, they must be able to recognize organizational patterns in informational text, such as sequential, cyclical, or hierarchical. They must be able to connect facts in a logical way. Research repeatedly demonstrates that students who do this recall more and comprehend better (Carrell, 1992; Moss, 1993; Pearson & Fielding, 1991; Taylor, 1992). Organizing also makes learning the information easier and more efficient.

Most elementary students are familiar with the organizing pattern of story structure. As discussed in Chapter 2, primary-grade children learn to identify this pattern through explicit teaching and immersion. As students become familiar with that pattern, it helps them to read almost all genres of fiction, such as folktales, mysteries, or realistic fiction. However, that is not the case for nonfiction, since nonfiction can be organized around so many different patterns.

Marcia Freeman (2003b) makes this distinction:

- Fiction is written in *chronological order* to show passage of time (therefore each story is similarly organized).

- Nonfiction is usually organized in *clumps of related information* (similar information is chunked together in various ways).

Reading information proficiently requires looking for those clumps of related information and making connections among those clumps to form concepts (Spiro & Taylor, 1987). This kind of conceptual understanding is what separates proficient readers from basic readers (see chart page 158).

The goal here is for children to become aware of organizing patterns of information. Fourth grade may be too late. Since we begin assessing for this skill nationally and statewide in fourth grade (and even in third grade in many states), it is important to lay the foundation for conceptual understanding early in the primary grades.

Andie Cunningham (Cunningham & Shagoury, 2005) begins in kindergarten. She teaches her students about uncovering "special ideas that are hidden." And she is right on target. Ideas and concepts are hidden because they are *between the facts*. Our job as teachers is to expose those ideas—to explicitly show our primary students how to look for patterns, relationships, and chunks of information to infer those ideas.

This is not easy. Research shows students have a difficult time organizing information on their own (Kintsch, 1998; McGee & Richgels, 1982; Walpole, 1998). Try handing a highlighter to third graders and

Organizing Information Makes Learning Easier and More Efficient

➜ Readers access information randomly when they are unaware of the organization (Lapp, Flood, & Farnan, 1996). Most children don't even think about information being organized. They read for isolated facts.

➜ When facts are dealt with in isolation, the brain stores them differently and requires more practice and rehearsal of the information (Caine & Caine, 1991). It is more difficult to learn isolated information.

➜ When readers cannot see relationships, they have difficulty retaining information.

(Bransford, Stein, Shelton, & Owings, 1981; Macken-Horarik, 2002; McGee & Richgels, 1982)

Proficient Readers:	Basic Readers:
◆ Look for what is important in a text ◆ Look for how information is related ◆ Look for how information is organized ◆ Look for signals in text to find how information is organized ◆ Connect information to prior knowledge and categorize it ◆ Store information in long-term memory	◆ Pay attention to what interests them in the text ◆ Pull out information for interest, not for importance to understanding overall meaning ◆ Read for facts and not relationships among facts ◆ Do not look for how information is organized ◆ Store information in short-term memory only

asking them to highlight only the important concepts—they tend to mark up the entire page! Students don't automatically see relationships or patterns to figure out the key concepts (Caine & Caine, 1991), and years of being taught to think in parts hasn't helped (Cuban, 1993; Myers, 1996; Senge et al., 2000).

However, when students are taught to organize, they increase both comprehension and writing skills (Lapp et al., 1996; McGee & Richgels, 1982). I have seen and experienced success in classroom after classroom, as teachers have explicitly taught students how to think conceptually by organizing information.

Early in the year in Beth's classroom, for example, her students had just reread an informational text about famous paintings from their fine arts curriculum. This simple text shows examples of different paintings. Notice how the children are drawn to the isolated facts.

BETH: Let's think about our book we just read. What is this book about?

JOSIAH: The author plays tricks on us? [Notices one of the pages in which the author provided an optical illusion]

MACY: That was the orange window.

BETH: Well, in one picture the author did! But was that what the whole book was about? The orange window was only one part. But I'm talking about the whole book. [Outstretches her arms to show she is talking about the concept for the entire book]

JERELL: The cows are fighting.

BETH: In one painting we saw that the cows were fighting. But was the *whole* book about cows fighting?

To figure out what the whole book was about, the children had to think about how each page is related—to look at the parts and then determine the "special hidden idea," the concept, by looking at how those parts are related. As Beth worked with her first graders throughout the year, they learned to connect facts to think conceptually.

By spring, her students had sorted, chunked, and looked for patterns within informational texts multiple times. They participated in lively and engaging conversations as they evaluated the information for conceptual understanding.

BETH: Let's look up here. Let's think about the book that we just read about the solar system. I'm going to give you information to think about. Look at this: Here's Mercury, Venus, Earth, and Mars. Did order matter with this information?

MARGO: Yes, because you can't go Venus, Earth, Mars, and Mercury. They said it is the hottest thing, and it would be closest to the sun.

BETH: So it started with the closest and went to the farthest? Why did order matter about the information in this book?

JOSEPH: It all travels around the sun and it makes night and morning.

LIZZIE: It *depends* on if order matters. It depends on what you want to know. If you want to know facts from the closest to the not closest, but if you don't care you can skip around. [Knows that there is more than one way to organize information]

BETH: You are right! We can organize the planets in different ways. But we are looking to see how this author put the information together in this book. How did he organize the information?

MACY: He put it closest to not the closest.

MARGO: He could have just mixed them up.

BETH: So why do you think he put them in this order?

MATT: To make it a true story.

JENNA: So we would know which one was next to the other.

BETH: So what do you think he is telling us about?

JOSEPH: This is the *whole* solar system, not just the planets.

CHLOE: In the solar system the planets are in order.

MARGO: But in the book yesterday it was just a bunch of facts about the planets.

SEAN: On the front they showed the planets in order.

BETH: But when we opened and started reading, were they in order?

CHLOE: It was just a listing of facts about the planets.

Beth discovered that through modeling, explicit instruction, and practice her first graders were able to think between the facts to connect information. They could analyze an informational text for organizational patterns. They were creating conceptual understanding.

A Mind Picture for Evaluating Text for Conceptual Understanding

I use Legos® to introduce this strategy to students. We talk about how playing with Legos is a bit like learning information. I pour the Legos out onto the table and it seems to be an awful lot of small pieces—hundreds of pieces! All those pieces lying on the table are just potential constructions at this point— potential houses, cars, ships, castles. The pieces are really only useful once they are connected to other pieces.

In the same way, facts alone are just potential understanding. By themselves, they can be overwhelming and confusing. But they become clearer and more useful

Learning with Legos

when they are connected to other facts. Once I asked a group of third graders, "What good is one Lego piece by itself?" Taylor remarked, "It hurts when you leave it on the floor and step on it." When I asked them to compare building with Legos to learning facts, another child chimed in, "And it hurts when you have to learn facts also!" He had hit the nail on the head. When you learn information as isolated facts, it hurts! However, when you learn how to connect the facts into chunks or organizing patterns, it makes it so much easier to learn, remember, and understand.

Creating With Legos	Creating Conceptual Understanding
You have to connect the pieces to make something.	You have to connect facts to make it easier to understand the information.
There are many different ways to put Legos together.	You can sort and map facts in different ways to organize them.
You can create many different things with the same set of Legos. Different people might build different stuff from the same Legos.	You can use the same set of facts and find different ways to connect them. Not everyone will connect facts in the same way.
When you've had lots of practice with using Legos, it gets easier and easier.	The more that you sort and map facts, the easier and easier it gets.
If you know how to do it, you can build from your own imagination; if you don't, you need to follow the directions.	If you know how to sort and use maps, you can make your own. But if you don't, the teacher can help you know how to do it.
Directions usually come in the box of Legos so that you can use them if you need them.	The teacher gives you directions at the beginning so that you know how to put the facts together.
Legos by themselves aren't very useful; they must be connected to be useful.	Facts by themselves are hard to learn. They are better when connected to other facts.
You can't just connect them any old way; they have to go together to make something.	You can't just put any facts together; they have to go together (be related).
Sometimes just trying out something gives you ideas about how to build.	The more you sort and arrange facts in different ways, the more ideas you get.

Proficient readers can pick up a text and begin building understanding from the facts since they know how to connect them. Basic readers need step-by-step instruction in how to connect facts until they are more able and ready to do it on their own. With instruction, they will learn that information is most useful when it is connected to other information. They will also discover that there are many different ways to organize the same set of facts.

And soon they will be able to visualize how the parts fit together as they read, evaluating information conceptually and, therefore, competently.

Teaching Evaluating Text for Conceptual Understanding: A Way to Introduce and Develop the Strategy

Graphic organizers are powerful visual tools for seeing relationships and key concepts (Bromley, Irwin-DeVitis, & Modlo, 1995; Hyerle, 1996; Moline, 1995). However, for children to build conceptual understanding using graphic organizers, they must develop some foundational thinking skills: to see relationships, make categories, and identify patterns. This section provides tools to help children develop those skills. Specifically, it contains:

- Tools for sorting information into chunks

- Tools for mapping out connections among chunks

- Tools for identifying big-picture patterns

Tools for Sorting Information Into Chunks

Beth brought several toiletries from home, such as shampoo, toothpaste, shaving cream, and lotion. As she pulled them out of the shopping bag and placed them on the rug in front of her first graders, she grouped certain items together and conducted a think-aloud.

BETH: If I wanted to organize these things from home, I would put things together that are alike. I would put these items together because they are all tubes. But these are cans and must go in a different group. Now if I wanted to group the items that come in bottles, what would I put together?

From there, her students jumped in to help her organize her items. She had them group items according to their color and shape, things that you could squeeze or not squeeze, and things you could use in the bathtub. Victor began to see the chunks (or categories) and how the items were related.

VICTOR: What about things that foam?

BETH: Which things do I need to put in front of me for things that foam?

VICTOR: Soap, shampoo, and toothpaste.

Beth: What makes you say soap?

Victor: Well, if you put it under the water and rub your hands, it makes foam. And when you brush your teeth, the toothpaste foams.

Victor was already looking to see how the different items might be related. Throughout the course of the following months, Beth used sorting in a variety of ways to help all her students learn to look for relationships, make categories, and see patterns.

Concepts are abstract labels given to identify the *rule of the relationship*. It is generalized thinking that is inferred from the specifics. For instance, shampoo, soap, and shaving cream are specifics that all fit into the general category (or concept) of "things that foam." As children sort, they look for reasons to categorize things that are alike or have similar attributes. As they talk through their decisions, they identify the rules for the categories, which are the concepts. They learn how to chunk information, which I have found helps them to identify chunks of information within text.

I introduce sorting in the following kid-friendly ways: follow-the-rule sorting, guess-the-rule sorting, and make-the-rule sorting. For each type, I move from closed sorts (in which the teacher identifies the categories) to open sorts (in which students identify the categories).

Follow-the-Rule Sorting

In follow-the-rule sorting, the teacher chooses one rule (or category) and the students find items that follow only that rule. Beth was doing follow-the-rule sorting in the above example. She gave the rule "things that come in bottles." Her students then sorted through the items to find only those that fell into that category.

It is best to begin with concrete, everyday items that children can physically sort. This enables them to focus on learning to look for similarities and differences rather than on learning a new concept. They can sort buttons, toys, clothes, or school supplies. Once students are comfortable sorting concrete, everyday items, move them to sorting cards with pictures representing concrete items, and eventually to cards with words representing items. Since it is a print-based activity, sorting word cards is a natural precursor to sorting information in text.

> ## Ideas for Follow-the-Rule Sorting
>
> → Sort familiar, concrete items such as buttons, toiletries, or toys.
>
> → Sort picture cards to represent items.
>
> → Sort word cards.

Sorting Word Cards Once children know how to sort concrete items, have them sort cards with pictures or words. Generate a list of items from the children using a familiar broad category (such as food, animals, weather words, etc.). From this *student-generated* list, create a set of cards for each group of three to five children to sort. Children do their sorting whole-group (as above), in small groups, or with partners. The same set of cards can be used for several sorting experiences.

Food "Rules" (or Categories)

→ fruit

→ meat

→ grains

→ dairy products

→ breakfast foods

→ lunch foods

→ cafeteria foods

→ foods for snacks

→ foods for dessert

→ favorite foods

→ holiday foods

→ grows on trees

→ grows in the ground

→ foods you like

→ sour foods

♦ Determine several categories that can be used for sorting. Call out only one rule (category), and have children sort through the cards to find items that "follow the rule." For instance, you might ask students to find foods that are "fruit" or "cafeteria foods" or "food that grows on trees." There should be only two piles: items that follow the rule and those that don't. Have children sort three to four different categories so that they can see how the same information can be sorted and organized in different ways.

♦ Teach students how to make decisions about sorting the cards into categories with their peers. As children sort and generalize, decisions will have to be made about which cards belong in which pile, and later they will have to make decisions about what to label each category. Children need to know how to work through the process of making those kinds of decisions. In these activities, the process of decision making is as important as the outcome. For instance, Tamra thought that "pizza" should be included in her group's "breakfast foods" pile. The group had to decide if it was okay to include the item if only one person ate pizza for breakfast or, rather, if it had to be a normal breakfast food for it to be included. Her group decided that as long as one of their group ate it for breakfast they would include it, no matter how weird it seemed! The rationale behind the decision is as critical as the outcome of the decision. These decisions will vary from group to group.

Food	Animals	Other Lists
♦ fruit	♦ with webbed feet	♦ winter activities
♦ dairy products	♦ with hooves	♦ summer activities
♦ vegetables	♦ with sharp claws	♦ signs of winter
♦ meat	♦ with feathers	♦ signs of spring
♦ grains	♦ with horns	♦ weather words
♦ lunch foods	♦ by number of legs	♦ things the wind does
♦ cafeteria foods	♦ wild/domesticated	♦ things found in each season
♦ food for snacks	♦ that are the same color	♦ clothes you wear in summer/winter
♦ breakfast foods	♦ that fly	
♦ foods you can make	♦ live in the forest	♦ things to do in each season
♦ foods for dessert	♦ live on the farm	♦ holidays
♦ smells good	♦ live in the ocean	♦ what happens in winter
♦ sour foods	♦ live in trees	♦ what happens in fall
♦ sweet foods	♦ live in our state	♦ what happens in spring
♦ foods eaten hot	♦ you can hold in your hand	♦ what happens in summer
♦ foods eaten cold	♦ larger than you	♦ how snow feels
♦ foods eaten raw	♦ that build nests	♦ things to do in the snow
♦ dry foods	♦ carry babies on their back	♦ what animals *cannot* do
♦ foods you like	♦ frighten you	♦ what you can do in a minute
♦ foods you don't	♦ oviparous	♦ what you can do in an hour
♦ favorite foods	♦ hibernate	♦ what you can do in a day
♦ holiday foods	♦ nocturnal	♦ short things/tall things
♦ grows on trees	♦ small animals	♦ things that scare you
♦ grows in ground	♦ medium animals	♦ things that grow/don't
♦ kinds of soup	♦ huge animals	♦ things at home/school

Sorting categories

- Have students talk to one another as they sort, as talk is imperative to sorting. Too often when given the task of sorting in a group, one of the students will pick up the stack of cards and begin sorting while the others simply watch and nod their heads in agreement. *Sorting should never be silent!* As students consider one rule at a time and find which items follow the rule, they must learn to talk to one another about why certain items follow the rule or do not. Through discussion they consider how things are alike and ways that things might be connected, or related. They learn to think aloud as they make decisions. If little talk is going on in the group, the power of the activity and the learning are diminished.

Sorting cards and categories they could fall under

- Provide sorting opportunities over several days, sorting three to four different categories each day. Using broad concepts (such as animals or food) allows you to use the same set of sorting cards for a couple of weeks.

Sorting Information Once children know how to sort general word cards, use text-specific words or facts from an informational text. Choose 10 to 20 words or facts from the text that can be sorted into different categories. Create a set of sorting cards for each group of children. After reading the text, give one category at a time for students to sort. Have groups discuss the information from the text as they sort. After each sort, have the groups share and discuss how and what they included in their category.

For example, in a third-grade social studies class, I used follow-the-rule sorting to help students better understand the more difficult concept of child labor. Using the *Scholastic News* article "The Cost of Child Labor" (Hayes, 1996), I chose about 30 words or phrases to make into sorting cards for each group (see chart page 167). I then created several categories that would facilitate the sorting and discussing of key concepts in the article.

Teaching the Information Generation

soccer	Asia	Central America	change	250 million	kids	sporting goods
.60¢	newspaper	Adidas	most powerful kid	$6.00	school	fields
Pakistan	Africa	$1,000,000	United States	$30.00	Unicef	ILO
New York	letters	Reebok	Nike	rugs	action	5–14

After reading the article, I asked the students to find information that would follow the rule for the concept of *places using child labor.* Students chose information they thought was related to the category, talking through their reasoning as they sorted. I encouraged them to refer to the article as they sorted. After the groups sorted, we revisited the article as a whole group to talk about what cards they had placed in their pile and their thinking behind their choices. This also allowed me to guide the discussion and clarify any misconceptions. A couple of groups included only countries; other

Students need to talk as they sort information.

groups included sporting goods companies as places because they contended that they had factories where the kids made the soccer balls and shoes. We continued in this format as the groups sorted the cards for other categories, one category at a time: *who is using child labor, what is being done to stop child labor, the children working in child labor, who is causing child labor, child labor outside the U.S.,* and *child labor inside the U.S.*

By sorting and re-sorting the information in various ways, students were able to see chunks of information within the article. New understandings about child labor developed. After sorting and discussing who was causing child labor, Noah exclaimed, "There's a card missing here. *We* should be included in here because we are buying

Rules for Sorting by Rules

→ Work in groups of three to five.

→ Model sorting and thinking out loud.

→ Encourage children to talk through their thinking as they sort.

→ **Make group decisions:** "What makes you say that?"

→ **Justify decisions:** Not just "what pile?" but "why in that pile?"

the soccer balls that Nike is selling that these kids are making!"

Guess-the-Rule Sorting

With guess-the-rule sorting, the teacher provides a set of related items and students must guess the rule—or category. They must consider all possible relationships—as there is usually more than one possible rule or category that will fit. This is a critical type of sorting for conceptual understanding, as it requires inferring a generalized idea from specifics. It is here that students are learning how concepts are created.

Sorting Word Cards To introduce this type of sorting, choose four to six related words. Place word cards in a pocket chart or write the words on the board. Have a specific category (rule) in mind. For example, I might place *apple, peach, pear,* and *plum* in the pocket chart. Children begin guessing the rule. As they guess, I ask everyone to check to make sure that the guess fits the rule. Children might guess: fruit, food that grows on trees, food in a salad, or food Mom puts in my lunch. (One child guessed, "Fruit that have the letter P"!) As we agree that the rule they guessed would work, I respond: "It fits the rule, but it's not my rule," until children have guessed the rule in my head (food with skin).

After Beth took her first graders on a field trip to the farmer's market, she created a guess-the-rule sorting activity. The class first came up with a list of all the fruits and vegetables they had seen at the farmer's market. Then each child created a card with a picture of one of the fruits or vegetables and labeled the food. From this, they made a class sorting set. Beth called the children to the floor in small groups. She sorted the cards into piles on the floor and had the group guess the rule for the categories she created.

Sorting Information After several opportunities for learning how to guess the rule, apply this type of sorting to informational text. Choose 15 to 20 words or phrases from the text. Sort the information into categories on the board or in a pocket chart for students. Invite them to "guess the rule" to figure out the concept. Have them try to figure out how the items are related: "Why do you think I put giraffes, zebras, and lions in this column and fish, snakes, and chickens in this column? Can you guess the rule from what we read? How are these related"? [babies born alive and babies hatched from eggs].

As children have more practice in guessing the rule, have them begin to label the categories at their tables. As you pull four to six cards for the pocket chart, have them pull the same cards at their table. Then provide sticky notes for each group. As students talk, have them write down the rule they guess. As groups share, talk through why they guessed the rule.

Guessing the rule is often a difficult activity for children initially, but a necessary one in order for students to be able to determine "the special hidden ideas," or the key concepts. Children need multiple opportunities for this type of inferencing.

Beth guides a guess-the-rule sorting activity.

Make-the-Rule Sorting

After children have had sufficient practice with following the rule and guessing the rule, they are ready to determine rules and make their own rules. In other words, they are ready to carry out open sorts. From a set of word cards, students sort the information into categories of their choice. The groups determine how the information is connected and create categories from the relationships. Students label their categories with sticky notes. After sorting, groups share their thinking.

Beth had each of her students write a fact from their book about ladybugs on a sentence strip. The students sat around the carpet as Beth guided them to sort the facts into categories, or to "make the rule":

TriBond

Children need lots of support in learning how to "guess the rule." TriBond (or TriBond, Jr.) by Mattel is a board game that helps me provide that support. Students have to think in threes to solve riddles. For example, what do an elephant, a car, and a tree have in common? (A trunk.) Rather than playing the board game, I pull the cards and ask one riddle each day. As students think about what these items have in common, they are learning to make connections between objects—a critical skill for reading informational text and an NAEP literacy expectation.

BETH: I have some facts about ladybugs that you wrote. We're going to sort them and see if any of them go together.

The class read through their ladybug facts spread around in the middle of the carpet.

> Some ladybugs eat aphids and some eat plants.
> Ladybugs can lay 100 eggs.
> Ladybugs have four stages to grow.
> Ladybugs eat aphids, mealy bugs, and plants.
> Ladybugs have spots, wings, and six legs.
> Ladybugs protect themselves with their bright colors.
> Ladybugs get together to hibernate.
> Ladybugs have spots on them.
> Ladybugs can lay 100 eggs in a day.
> Ladybugs eat aphids.
> Ladybugs lay eggs.
> There are over 400 different kinds of ladybugs.
> Ladybugs eat aphids and they eat pests.
> Ladybugs are usually red and yellow.
> Ladybugs have a mom and dad.

BETH: Who can help me see which ones go together? Which ones are related?

JENNA: Well, they eat aphids and they eat pests.

BETH: So we can put these facts together. [Picks up the sentence strips and sorts them into a pile]

BETH: Is there another one that can go in that pile?

CHRIS: I see one.

ZOE: Here is another, "Ladybugs eat aphids."

BETH:	What is the same about all these? [Holds up strips] What can we call this category? What is our rule for putting these in this pile?
ANNA:	They are all what they eat.
BETH:	So we can call it "What ladybugs eat." Are there any other facts that go in this category?

Beth wrote the name of the category on an index card and placed it on the top of the pile of facts. These first graders soon were finding other categories, sharing their thinking, and turning facts into conceptual understanding.

MARGO:	I thought of another group.
BETH:	What is that, Margo?
MARGO:	Eggs. Look, there is "Ladybugs can lay 100 eggs" and "Ladybugs lay eggs." They both tell about eggs.
BETH:	So let's keep these together. Anything else that goes with this group?
NICHOLAS:	The mom and the dad.
BETH:	What makes you say the mom and dad goes with the eggs?
NICHOLAS:	It's the family, and that's who lays the eggs.
CHLOE:	I think this one goes. "Ladybugs have four stages to grow."
BETH:	Now what makes you say that?
CHLOE:	Because they lay eggs and that is one of the stages.
BETH:	So if we are going to put the four stages in with the other facts about eggs, what can we call this group? We need to make sure that we tell how they all go together.
GABRIELLE:	How they grow.
BETH:	Great idea! What makes you choose that one?
GABRIELLE:	It tells how they start and then how they grow.
MARGO:	They start with eggs.
BETH:	Good thinking! Let's read our text again and see if anything else goes with how they grow.

Tools for Mapping Out Connections Among Chunks

Graphic organizers are powerful for helping children see and represent chunks of information. They show how the information is related—and how the facts can be categorized to create concepts (Bromley et al., 1995; Hyerle, 1996; Moline, 1995). This is not new news about graphic organizers, I realize. Most of us have been using them for years. But what I've learned recently is the importance of *how* we use them. We can't just pull them from the teacher's guide, hand them to students, and expect learning to occur. We must teach students how to use them in interactive, collaborative ways to build thinking skills.

When introducing graphic organizers, I use the analogy of a map. I ask students to consider that a map visually demonstrates the location of places in the world, showing the connections and relationships of those places to one another. Looking at a map I might ask: "What is the relationship of New Orleans to New York? Where are they located in relation to each other?" Graphic organizers allow students to map chunks of information to show connections and relationships among those chunks. It is often in the process of mapping information that conceptual understanding occurs. This is why I use the term "graphic organizer maps," or "GO maps" as my students called them.

Types of Organizers

Karen Bromley (Bromley et al., 1995) has identified four basic "patterns of knowledge organization" that have proved powerful in my work with teachers and students. These organizational patterns are based on the different ways that information is related. Students can map any kind of information with GO maps for each pattern: *concept, hierarchical, sequential,* and *cyclical* (Bromley et al., 1995). Although Bromley classifies the Venn diagram as a type of conceptual organizer (comparing two concepts), I have found it less confusing for young children just to introduce it as a fifth type of organizational pattern.

Mapping as Representation

Children learn how to link information with GO maps. These GO maps can be created in the last column of the Go! Chart, which is labeled "Organizing." (See Chapter 3 for more on GO! Charts.) The concept map is the first organizer that I introduce to students.

Teaching the Information Generation

Types of Organizers	Basic Ways to Organize Information
Concept Map	A conceptual organizer is the most common type of graphic organizer used in the classroom. The concept (the rule) is in the middle of the map, with supporting facts or details listed around the concept. This framework reflects the relationship of the facts to the concept. Best map to use when simply making a list.
Venn Map	When comparing two concepts, the concept maps overlap, forming a Venn diagram, showing similar and different characteristics.
Hierarchical Map	A hierarchical framework organizes information in a ranking order, identifying the main concept (superordinate concept), and then levels of subconcepts (subordinate concepts), and facts or details underneath. The ranks move from top to bottom because of the level of importance or abstraction. Best to use when an organized list is needed.
Sequential Map	When events are related chronologically or in a linear way, they are represented by a sequential map. This GO map visually shows the relationship of each event to the next; this would include such relationships as cause-effect, problem-solution. Best organizer to use with temporal (time-ordered) or causal (cause-and-effect) relationships.
Cyclical Map	This framework is similar to the sequential pattern in that the events are related in a chronological order; however, a cyclical framework represents a continuous sequence of events or a series of events that begin and end in the same place.

The concept map shows a list of items related to a concept. Order of the information is not important. There are several ways to introduce GO maps, including mapping sorts, mapping with sticky notes, and mapping a "fist list" (Freeman, 2000), and all work well with the concept map.

This kindergartener is using a concept map.

Mapping Sorts After sorting word cards, model how to apply the sort to a simple GO map. For example, a group of third graders had sorted the category of breakfast foods. I modeled how to map the sort with a graphic organizer. I recorded the category (the rule) in the middle of a circle on the board and then listed the foods in the sort around the circle, attaching each food to the circle with a line. I introduced the term "concept" as the label for the category, showing them that we had created a *concept map.* Each group recorded their sort as a concept map. Students learn to sort and then record sorts to visually show the category and the relationship with a simple concept map.

Mapping With Sticky Notes Children write or draw their facts on a sticky note and then place them on a chart around the category listed in the middle. I was using this activity with a group of first graders to introduce mapping. After we read the text *Chickens Aren't the Only Ones* (Heller, 1999), we listed all the animals in the book that laid eggs. Each child chose one animal to record on a small sticky note. I did a think-aloud: "How could we show that each of these animals that you wrote on your sticky note lays eggs? Let's map it out to show that. Let me draw a large circle up here and write, 'Animals that lay eggs.' This is our category. Now only animals that lay eggs can be added to our circle." The children came up and added their sticky notes around the outside of the circle. "Let's draw a line from each sticky note to the category so that we can show that each fact is related to our category, which is also called a 'concept.' Each fact is connected to our concept, which is why we call this kind of map a 'concept map.' "

Mapping a "Fist List" This is a great concrete tool for young readers. When mapping a category, have children make a "fist list" (Freeman, 2000): Their fist represents the category and their fingers represent each fact that is related to the category. As children make a fist, label the category. "My fist is like the category of 'animals that lay eggs.' But that doesn't tell me which animals lay eggs. Let's name some of the animals that we know." As you name the animal, raise a finger. "A chicken lays eggs." [Raises index finger] "A snake lays eggs." [Raises middle finger] "A duck lays eggs." [Raises ring finger] "An octopus lays eggs." [Raises little finger] "And a bird lays eggs." [Raises thumb] Then show children how they can record their fist list as a concept map. Their fist is like the circle in the middle and their fingers are the details that are connected to the category.

By introducing mapping in these concrete ways, you show children how you are recording information that is connected. They come to understand the category, or the rule, as the big idea and its subcategories. They are learning to map relationships.

Determining Which Kind of Map to Use

Children need to know how to make decisions about which kind of GO map to use for different kinds of information. *Does order matter?* is a simple, yet profound, question that helps young readers discern organizational patterns. As children consider this question, it simplifies the process for determining how to map the information.

♦ If order doesn't matter, choose a *concept map* or a *hierarchical map.*

♦ If order matters, choose a *sequential map* or a *cyclical map.*

♦ If you are comparing or contrasting information, choose a *Venn map* or a *hierarchical map.*

Students most likely need at least 15 meaningful exposures to a strategy, with guidance and practice, before it is internalized (Ellis, 1997, 2004). It works well to introduce one type of organizational pattern and then continue to model and reinforce that pattern with five to six other informational texts until students become familiar with the organizational pattern. Then introduce the other patterns one at a time in a similar format.

Over the course of the school year, be sure to introduce each of the organizational patterns to your students, giving them ample opportunity to see you model mapping and then for them to integrate the maps into their own reading and eventually use them

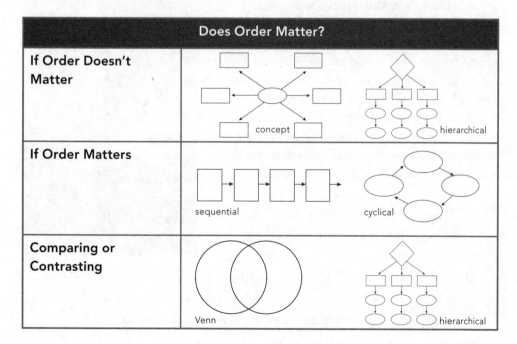

---

in their writing. Soon students will be helping you map the information. In fact, Brandi reported that now her kindergarten students love to map just about everything!

Teachers have found that hanging a large chart with all five organizers in their classroom to be helpful as they teach children how to map information. See the appendix Ways to Organize Information (page 216) for a sample chart that can be enlarged for classroom use.

Tools for Identifying Big-Picture Patterns

Although there are a variety of ways that informational text can be organized, there is one pattern you'll see used in all types, regardless of organization: *beginning, middle,* and *end.* As students learn to evaluate information conceptually, they need to think about this pattern so that they can apply what they learn to their reading and writing. Here are three activities that will help them to do that: the house visual organizer, the take-apart-and-chart activity, and the Author's Message Plan.

House Visual Organizer

Think about the house in which you live, have lived, or would like to live. Although you spend most of your time, effort, and energy in the middle, a house is not complete unless it has a roof to cover it and a foundation to stand on. "What would happen if there wasn't a roof over your house? What if there wasn't a foundation?" I ask children. A house must include all three parts to be solid.

Beth used this organizer with her first graders often to represent the three parts of an informational text—and you can tell by their conversation!

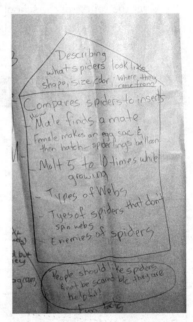

This is a sample house organizer.

BETH:	If I draw the house . . .
DAKOTA:	You want to show the different parts.
JOSEPH:	Because it's easy to remember the house.
MARGO:	Because you can draw a picture of a house and you see houses.
BETH:	You are right. What are the different parts?

Teaching the Information Generation

MARGO: The beginning is the big part, and the end is the big part, and the little parts are all in the middle.

The roof represents the beginning of the text, since it "covers" the information. The first few sentences tell the reader what the text is about, the big idea. The author usually provides a "hook" or a real-life connection for the reader.

LIZZIE: The roof is the big thing.

BETH: That is like the beginning. What is the job of the beginning?

ZOE: It's the big topic.

MATT: It gets your mind ready to read.

KYLE: And it helps you understand.

The inside of the house represents the middle of the text, since it is where most of the information is and where the reader will spend most of his time and energy. This is where the information is organized in chunks or patterns: *conceptual, hierarchical, sequential,* or *cyclical.*

BETH: What is the job of the middle of the text? What does it do?

ZOE: It's the little things.

MARGO: The facts.

SEAN: The little things you need to know.

BETH: So the middle tells us all the new information that we will learn.

The foundation represents the end of the text—a firm place upon which to wrap up ideas. The author usually takes the reader back to the big picture.

BETH: What about the end of a text?

CHLOE: It has to go back to the beginning.

MARGO: It goes back to the big idea.

BETH: Why do we need an end?

ANNA: If it didn't have an end, the story would never end.

CHRIS: It helps make your mind close at the end. You're done.

BETH: So the end goes back to what the author said in the beginning. To the big idea.

To use this analogy with students, draw a simple picture of a house on chart paper or the board.

- Draw a red roof and foundation and then blue lines for the walls. Color coding the beginning and ending helps children to visually identify these parts.

- Read the beginning of the text and think aloud with the children: "How can we put in our own words what the author was telling us in the beginning?"

- Write in the roof (or just outside the roof) the big idea concept given in the beginning. Paraphrasing is critical here. Do not copy from the text!

- Read the information in the middle. Evaluate the information with the students. How is it organized? What graphic organizer can best be used with this kind of information? Model how to organize the information into a GO map. Create the map inside the house.

- Read the end of the text. Evaluate how the author wrapped up the text. Paraphrase at the bottom of the house.

How does the beginning signal the reader?
Look for connections the author shares.
Look for clues the author gives about the information to come.

What kind of information does the middle tell the reader?
Look to see how the information is organized.
Figure out what kind of GO map would best show that.

How does the end signal the reader?
Look to see how the author takes the reader back to the big idea.

The house organizer helps children "see" if they include beginning, middle, and end.

The house organizer has proven powerful for evaluating informational text. Children have successfully transferred this visual to their own reading to see the global pattern, and eventually used it to help structure their own writing.

Take Apart and Chart

Evaluating informational text for beginning, middle,

and end is about learning to see the big picture organization. However, young readers often have not developed the thinking skills required for this type of holistic evaluation. A take-apart-and-chart activity helps children concretely see the text as a whole and figure out if order matters.

In this activity, the teacher "takes apart" an informational text by writing down the main facts (or concepts) on sentence strips; the beginning of the text also is written on a separate sentence strip, as is the ending. These are all placed in a pocket chart. Color-coding the sentence strips helps young readers to identify the three parts of the text. The beginning and ending strips are written in red marker and the main facts from the middle are written in blue marker. Sticky notes can be used to label beginning, middle, and end. Brandi used the parts of the house (roof, walls, floor) on sticky notes to show her kindergartners the correlation of the take-apart activity to the house diagram.

Beth guides a take-apart-and-chart activity.

Children then manipulate the facts in the pocket chart, changing the order of the information. I point out to them that they cannot change the red strips (the beginning and the end), as those will always stay the same. The beginning is always the beginning and the end is always the end! They soon learn to anticipate these two parts of the text. Eventually drop the color coding and sticky notes as children learn to identify the beginning, middle, and ending pattern.

At the heart of this activity is the manipulation of the facts. Children change the order of the facts and then the class reads the facts again, thinking, Does order matter? Discuss the facts with children and how they go together, and determine if order was important to the information.

Beth found this activity to work well at the end of the Go! Chart format, to wrap up the week's work with an informational text. The class read the facts in the pocket chart from *Chickens Aren't the Only Ones* (Heller, 1999). Isaac came to the pocket chart and changed the order of the strips.

Jenna:	Yes, order matters. Now they're mixed up.
Beth:	What makes you say yes, Jenna?
Jenna:	Because, yes, when chickens hatch it can't hatch in four days because it's not ready. And it can't be out of its egg when it's not ready.

MARGO: Because it can't go fourteen days and then four days because it would shrink.

BETH: So you are saying that order matters because you can't go from fourteen days to four days, right?

NICHOLAS: That's the way it grows.

CHRIS: So the chicken can't get smaller! You don't want to go back, huh?

ZOE: It tells how the chicken hatches.

BETH: So order matters with the life cycle of the chicken. Let's put the facts back in the correct order.

Take-Apart-and-Chart Activity

1. Read an informational text to students.

2. List facts on sentence strips.

3. Place strips in pocket chart.

4. Label beginning, middle, and end.

5. Have students rearrange strips.

6. Ask: Does order matter?

7. Talk about the information.

8. Determine if order is important to the information.

9. Figure out which organizer works best to map the information.

After determining if order matters, model which type of organizer could be used to map the information. Beth and the class decided to use the sequential map to show the life cycle of the chicken. She created a sequential map in the last column of the Go! Chart they had been working with all week.

The sentence strips in this activity allow children to manipulate the facts and to see the parts of the global pattern. As the take-apart activity is used more and more, children come to anticipate the structure and to expect a beginning, middle, and end pattern. And they are able to recognize when parts of the global pattern are missing.

MARGO: Hey, there wasn't a beginning. There wasn't a question or anything.

ZOE: It doesn't have to have a question.

BETH: But what does a beginning have to do? What is the job of the beginning?

Teaching the Information Generation

SEAN:	It has to get our mind ready to think about what we will read.
BETH:	So did this text do that? Is this a beginning? [Points to the first sentence strip]
ANNA:	No, it just jumps right to the facts.
MARGO:	It doesn't have a beginning. That's not a beginning.
BETH:	So what would be a good beginning?
CHRIS:	Here are some facts about roosters and hens.
MARGO:	Did you know a rooster mates with a hen to make chickens?
SEAN:	Here are some facts about how you get a chick.
LIZZIE:	Here are some facts about chickens.
BETH:	I like how you went back to the big idea of the whole thing, Lizzie. The big idea is chickens, so we need a beginning about chickens. What do you think the author is trying to tell us?

Beth took the opportunity to take a blank sentence strip and to write a beginning sentence crafted by these first graders. Matt wanted to know, "How did this guy get to be an author if he didn't even know to put a beginning!"

Eventually students don't need the take-apart-and-chart activity. They will be able to see the text as a whole and to mentally think about how the facts are related. Consider Beth's class later in the semester.

BETH:	Let's look up here. We're going to take our text about ladybugs apart so that we can decide if order is important.
MARGO:	It doesn't matter.
BETH:	And you know that already?
CHLOE:	Because it is just telling us facts about ladybugs.
MARGO:	You can change them in any way and order doesn't matter.
BETH:	How do you know that?
MARGO:	Like you can say, "They're red and yellow." Then you can say, "They eat aphids." Order doesn't matter.
LIZZIE:	Order doesn't matter with a bunch of facts.
JOSEPH:	We're smart!
BETH:	Yes, you are so smart!

Author's Message Plan

The Author's Message Plan (AMP) is to be a "visual summary" of the process for evaluating a text. It is intended to help make students' thinking explicit as well as identify the signals the author provides in the text for evaluating organization.

The Author's Message Plan is divided into three main sections (*content, organization, and text signals*) and is charted on chart paper, or can be incorporated into the last column of the Go! Chart. Use the questions from each section to guide the discussion for evaluating the text. Then record responses, emphasizing how to paraphrase the author's words rather than copying from the text.

Title: _____	
Author: _____	
CONTENT	◆ What kind of information is the author sharing? ◆ How can I tell that in my own words?
ORGANIZATION	◆ Does order matter? ◆ How is the information related? ◆ How should I map it out? ◆ Can we show beginning, middle, and end?
TEXT SIGNALS	◆ What clues (or signals) did I find? ◆ What features were important to understanding the information?

Author's Message Plan

Teaching the Information Generation

Content: What kind of information is the author sharing in this text? The Author's Message Plan was a staple in Beth's first-grade classroom. It went hand-in-glove with the take-apart-and-chart activity. Each week, after completing the take-apart, she would create a Message Plan with her students.

BETH:	What kind of information is the author sharing in our text about planets? I want to write down in my own words what this book is about. I know that the author is telling me about planets because our title tells us that. But how can I say that in my own words? Why do you think the author wrote this book about planets?
JENNA:	To tell you about space.
BETH:	And how did he do that?
MARGO:	He described the planets.
SEAN:	Told us facts about the different planets.

The purpose of this first section is to push students to put the big idea into their own words rather than reading or regurgitating the information. Paraphrasing is essential. Beth wrote, "The author describes different planets."

Organization: How is the information related? How can we map the information?

BETH:	We have to decide if it had a beginning, middle, and end.
JOSEPH:	The beginning told us all about the solar system.
ZOE:	Everything that's in it.
BETH:	What is the job of the beginning?
CHRIS:	Gives us the big idea.
BETH:	So let's write the big idea of this text. "The solar system includes the sun, the planets, and their moons."

Beth used capital letters (BME) to distinguish beginning, middle, and end on the Author's Message Plan. They paraphrased what the author said in the beginning and the end on the chart. Then they evaluated the information about planets from the middle of the text.

BETH:	Did order matter? Which organizer can I use?
JOSEPH:	This one. [Points to chart on wall]
BETH:	The concept map. Good.
JOSEPH:	That one looks like the sun. The sun will be in the middle and then the planets will be listing parts.
MARGO:	Or we can use this one [Points to hierarchical map].
BETH:	So if I use the hierarchical map, what do I have to put at the top?

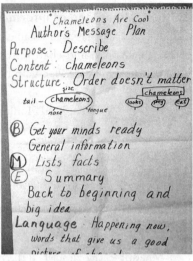

Here is an example of an Author's Message Plan.

LIZZIE:	"The Planets."
MARGO:	"Solar System."
BETH:	Planets is probably better because this section of our book doesn't talk about the Milky Way or the sun. It just talks about the planets in our solar system. What would I put here in the boxes?
LIZZIE:	Earth.
KYLE:	Mercury.
CHRIS:	Mars.

Joseph suggested they could use a concept map, since order didn't matter with this information. However, because the text talked about different planets, they decided to organize the list with a hierarchical organizer. Beth recorded each of the planets in the boxes on the hierarchical map and students offered facts to include about each planet. She listed the fact beneath the appropriate planet.

Text Signals: What clues (or text signals) did we find that helped us understand the information? This section of the AMP is intended to help students identify the clues or signals in the text that they used to evaluate the organization of the information. *How did you know that order mattered? Didn't matter? What signals did the author give to let us know?* These text signals might include steps, numbered photos, diagrams, or headings (access features). *Were there any diagrams with numbers? Photos that showed order?*

Patterns	Text Signals
Conceptual Pattern or Hierarchical Pattern	for example for instance most important *a list of characteristics or examples*
Venn Pattern or Hierarchical Pattern	like/unlike similarly but in contrast on the other hand however not only/but also as well as while although
Sequential Pattern or Cyclical Pattern	first, second, third, etc. next then last finally when following not long after before then after that because since as a result leads to so

Text signals for organizing information

Were there clues in the headings about the organization?

Authors sometimes use signal words that can clue the reader in to how the information is organized (order words, cause-and-effect words, comparing words, etc.). These types of signal words are charted in the last section of the Message Plan (see chart page 185). Students become aware of these types of signals and begin to look for them as they read.

In wrapping up the Author's Message Plan, have students summarize the information in their own words. "What do you think the author was trying to tell us in this informational text?" Children need to take the visual summary and translate it into an oral summary using their own language.

Of course, one of the best ways to demonstrate organizational patterns is by example. So use good examples of published informational texts. Informational texts for young children have clearer organizational patterns than books for older students. At the primary level, an entire book is usually organized around one concept with one organizational pattern. The entire book is about making a spider's web, or how a volcano forms, or different animals that live in a tree. However, as the content becomes more complex in the upper grades, the text also becomes more complex. Readers need to be aware that the organizational pattern may shift and change as the information shifts from section to section in a text. It is important to make this explicit to young readers. Different information in the same book may require different ways to organize.

Trying Out Evaluating Text for Conceptual Understanding: Ideas for Helping Students Apply the Strategy to Reading and Writing

As children become familiar with the different tools for organizing information, they need to try out the strategy with their own reading and writing. Primary students— including special education students—are capable of mapping all kinds of information: from how to make pizza to what polar bears eat. In this section I share ideas for helping children to learn to:

♦ Map their reading for conceptual thinking

♦ Map their writing to reflect conceptual thinking

Mapping Reading for Conceptual Thinking

Children sometimes have difficulty moving into conceptual thinking on their own. They may participate when the teacher is guiding the lesson and creating the shared GO map. But when left to their own devices, they have a hard time determining which information from a text is important and how to map it. Sorting saves the day!

Sorting to Organize Thinking When Reading

To help students learn to determine importance in a text, have them write the information they will sort. This differs from earlier sorts, when the teacher determined what facts to sort. Students work with partners or in small groups to write and sort facts from an informational text. In the opening scenario of the chapter, Debbie Sterling's second graders had read a text about Jane Goodall's work with chimps. Debbie had worked with her students for several days using the Go! Chart format. Partners worked together to determine what facts they thought were important. They wrote the facts (in their own words—no copying!) onto small sentence strips. The groups sorted their facts into categories and labeled the categories with sticky notes. After, Debbie had each set of partners share their categories and their thinking. One group had different piles for what Jane Goodall did. Another group listed the categories as "childhood, studying the chimps, teaching about the chimps." Some groups had "beginning, middle, and end of Jane Goodall's life."

From their categories, the partners map out the information using one of the GO maps. Using their GO map, partners orally retell the information to each other. *Nonfiction retellings should begin with a GO map.* Children need to visually organize their thinking before they can learn to mentally organize

Debbie's students sort facts about Jane Goodall.

Sorting to Organize Thinking

→ Write facts on strips of paper.

→ Sort facts into categories.

→ Label the categories.

→ Map the categories.

→ Retell the information.

thinking. As they listen to each other retell, the information should reflect the organization of the GO map and their own language. Have children use a checklist as they listen to their partner retell.

Using GO Maps to Organize Thinking When Reading

Sue Corey helped her second graders try out mapping with their own reading of informational text. She had done much explicit teaching and modeling during the first semester. Throughout the second semester she moved her students from more teacher-directed mapping to group mapping and independent mapping with their reading. She moved from texts with simple organization to more complex organizations within texts. Her journal, below, reflects what the students did and how they grew as readers and writers toward more conceptual thinking.

December 10	Used the cyclical map to have the children understand the water cycle. We glued four main pictures on a 12" x 18" piece of construction paper. Then the kids created the cyclical map around the pictures.	
January 4 **Martin Luther King Jr.**	Read book as group. Showed how to "take notes" using a sequential map. Children made their own sequential map. They were taught how to make notes into complete sentences and write a report on Martin Luther King Jr.	
February 1	Partner-read a small nonfiction book (chosen by teacher based on reading levels of the children). Then the group had to decide which map to use to retell the information. They created the map, then used it to tell the rest of the class about their book.	
February 15 **Abraham Lincoln** **George Washington**	Read both books aloud. Kids decided which map to use to retell. We drew on easel and filled in boxes with info from books. Then divided the class in half. One group did a paragraph on Abraham Lincoln, the other did George Washington.	

Teaching the Information Generation

March 4 *Drums: The Beat Goes On*	I used this book with my Level 24 readers. After reading, they had to decide which map they thought they should use to give details about this book. They used a conceptual map, since the book only covered one topic. They were each able to make their own conceptual map, and use it to orally tell what they had learned.	
April 11 *Saving Ben*	My advanced readers tackled this book all by themselves! They read it independently, then decided they would need a sequential map to retell it, since order mattered. They created the map independently and are in the process of writing their paragraphs, also independently!	
April 26 *Wild Weather*	We had a discussion of which map would be the correct one to use and it was decided that we should use the hierarchical map. I paired the students, a more able student with a less able student, so they could help each other … They worked for one hour! I feel they were very successful at this! I modeled for them how to take the information on the map and use it to create a paragraph.	

Teacher Sue Carey's journal

Notice that each time Sue had her students map out the information, they used the information in some way. Either her students retold the information orally or they had to write the information. It is important that students have a lot of practice orally retelling the information before we expect them to be able to write a paragraph or a retelling.

After many opportunities to guide students in using GO maps, Sue worked with her second graders to see that different chunks of information could be shared in one book. As they read *Pumpkins* (Farmer, 2004), the students paid close attention to the signals in each section. Sue divided her class into small groups and gave each group a section of the book to map. Two groups used a hierarchical map: one showed reasons to carve pumpkins, the other gave four kinds of pumpkins. The other two groups used sequential maps: one to show how to carve a jack-o'-lantern and the other to show how to grow a pumpkin. After each group made their GO map, they retold the information to the rest of the class.

The students were able to see how the organization of each section was different. Sue talked with her students about how they would have to shift their thinking about order with each heading and each section. They were able to see the clumps of information as they learned to create conceptual understanding.

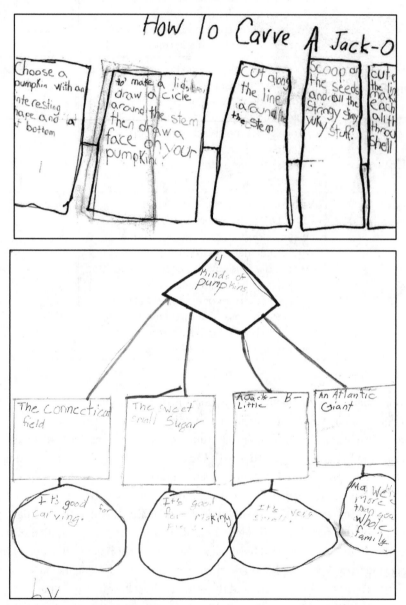

Sue's students used different GO maps to show different kinds of information about pumpkins.

Teaching the Information Generation

Mapping Writing to Reflect Conceptual Thinking

When reading an informational text, a proficient reader asks, "How did the author organize the information?" This helps the reader to create conceptual understanding to comprehend the content more deeply. When writing an informational text, a proficient writer asks, "How do I want to organize the information?" This helps the writer to write from conceptual understanding, reflecting his comprehension of the content.

As children need help and guidance to organize their thinking when reading, they also need experiences to learn how to organize their thinking for writing. Provide opportunities for talking, sorting, and mapping information before children write. Model how to organize your thinking before you create shared writings with your students. Provide opportunities for children to plan and share before they write. Expect organization when children write informational texts of their own. "Don't pick up a pencil before you have a plan" is an important motto. This section shares examples of how teachers have successfully done just that—and what a difference it has made in their student writing!

Create Class Books

Class books are a great way to share retellings and to provide opportunities for young writers to make decisions about how to organize information. Model how to sort and map the information before conducting a shared writing of the information. Beth created many class books of informational text over the course of the school year with her first graders.

She and her students had been reading about and studying birds and their beaks with the Go! Chart format. Each student drew a picture of one of the birds in their text. Beth guided their sorting on the carpet to organize the information for their class book.

BETH: How can we organize the information for our class book? Are there some birds that we should put together?

CHLOE: These all go together. They all eat nectar.

BETH: So Chloe says that these all go together. Let's see. She said the honeyeater, the lorikeet, and the hummingbird go together because . . .

LIZZIE: They all eat nectar.

BETH: What else should go together?

MATT: This and this one. We could put the seagull and the eagle because they are both white.

BETH: Are we sorting them by color? Let's look at the other category. What did we write about them?

MARGO: How they eat.

BETH: So let's look at how they eat. What else goes together?

ANNA: The pelican, the flamingo, and the oystercatcher.

BETH: What do they have in common?

ANNA: They all eat fish.

Beth continued to guide the conversation as they sorted, resorted, and continued discussing until all the birds were sorted into categories. Then they determined the label for each category. The discussion was lively, engaging, and collaborative.

BETH: So what are we going to call this category?

SEAN: Nectar drinkers.

BETH: Okay, what about this category?

LIZZIE: Fish eaters.

MATT: No, waterbirds.

BETH: What would be better? Tell me what you are thinking.

LIZZIE: I choose fish eaters because it is about what they eat. We aren't talking about "Oh, birds that swim in the water." We're talking about what they eat.

BETH: It does make sense to go with what they eat.

Once they had their chunks of information and labels for categories, Beth had the students determine the best way to map out their class book to write the information.

BETH: What kind of graphic organizer do we have to use to plan our book?

CHRIS: That one. [Points to chart on the wall]

BETH: What do we call that one?

CHLOE: Hierarchical.

BETH: What made you choose that one?

Teaching the Information Generation

CHRIS:	Because the big topic could be "what birds eat" and the little things tell what the birds eat.
BETH:	So under the big topic of "what birds eat" we have separate categories?
MATT:	Yeah, like fish, seeds, and insects.
MARGO:	We could list the categories, like honey, and then we could tell the birds that eat honey.
KYLE:	You can put the topic and then put the little facts underneath.
BETH:	So what should we call the big topic or the main idea? We have to write it at the top of our hierarchical map.
JENNA:	Bird food.
BETH:	Are we just talking about the food?
CHLOE:	About bird beaks.
JOSEPH:	How birds eat food.
MARGO:	But the really big idea is *how* birds live.
BETH:	You are saying that we need to say in our writing how birds get these kinds of food? So that their beak is important to getting this food? Let's remember that when we write our information.

From their sorting, talking, and mapping, these first graders were able to draw conclusions about the information to give a focus to their writing. They were ready to write about how birds get food with their beaks. As Beth conducted a shared writing, these first graders were able to write from a place of conceptual understanding.

Teach Beginnings and Endings

Young writers need to learn how to organize their writing with beginnings and endings. Conduct shared writing experiences modeling how to write effective beginnings and endings. Beth found that color-coding the organization of her shared writing to correlate with the house graphic helped her students transfer the organization to their own writing. She would use red marker to

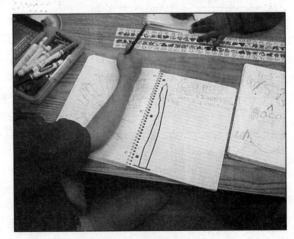

Children can use the house organizer to organize their informational writing.

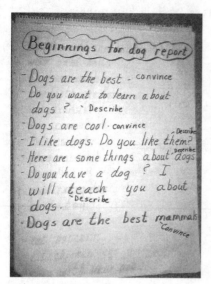

List of students' beginnings

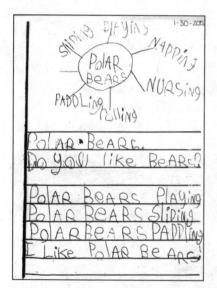

A kindergartener's writing with a
beginning, middle, and end

write beginnings and endings and blue for the middle
of the text. Then students would draw the house in
the margin of their writing to show their beginning,
middle, and end.

Model how to "hook" the reader in the beginning.
What would make them want to read my writing? Marcia
Freeman (2000) suggests that kindergarten and first-
grade writers use questions or exclamation hooks,
whereas second- and third-grade writers should expand
their writing repertoire to include a variety of devices.

An effective beginning also tells the reader what
the piece is about. *What is the big idea of this text?*
Brainstorm different ways to start a piece. Make a list of
two or three different ways to write the beginning and
let students choose which one works best.

As Beth's students said, "The ending goes back
to the beginning." It should wrap up the piece. *What
was this text about?* Have children try out different ways
to take the reader back to the big idea. Try asking a
question, or using an exclamation statement. Marcia
Freeman finds that writing endings is difficult for many
children, and suggests that they include how they
feel about the topic. See her book *Non-fiction Writing
Strategies* (2000) for further suggestions and ideas.

When modeling how to write an informational
text, let students know that most authors begin with
the middle, then go back and add the beginning and
ending. Freeman says, "There can be no effective
beginning or ending or transitions in a piece that is not
logically organized" (p. 22). Organizing the information
comes first. Once we know what we are going to write
about and how it is organized, then it is often easier to
write the beginning and the end. Ask any writer—the
beginning and the end are often the most difficult parts
to write! (See chart, next page, for suggestions.)

Teaching the Information Generation

Beginnings

→ Riddle or question

→ Exclamation or quotation

→ Talking directly to reader

→ Command

→ Rhyme or saying

→ A memory

→ Conversation or dialogue

→ A startling fact

→ Summary of key idea

→ Time or setting

→ Action

→ Definition

→ One word

→ Onomatopoeia

→ If . . .

→ Alliteration

Endings

→ Universal word

→ Question

→ Exclamation

→ Back to beginning

→ Interesting fact

→ Application

→ Author's response

→ Summarizing

→ Rhyme or saying

→ Comparison

Offer the Tools and Time to Write Informational Text

When Kyle came for a conference with Beth, he had written a short piece about sports below.

> I like to do soger [soccer].
> I like to do kroty [karate].
> I like to do gimnacs [gymnastics].
> I like to do sports.

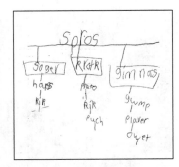

Kyle's organizing map

Beth talked with Kyle about his organizing map and realized he didn't have one. Kyle had not yet tried out the strategy of organizing on his own, so together they decided which kind of organizer map would work best for his writing. Kyle decided a hierarchical map would work, as he had three things he was going to write about: soccer, karate, and gymnastics. As Kyle mapped out his thinking, Beth asked him what he wanted to share about each of those sports. He listed on his map as he talked with Beth (see map, previous page). After talking, mapping, and planning, Kyle returned to his seat to write. Within the next 30 minutes, he wrote (invented spelling has been corrected for this sample):

> I like to do sports. I do soccer and karate, and don't forget gymnastics.
> At soccer you keep your hands down, and kick with your foot.
> At karate we practice and learn kicks. We practice punches.
> At gymnastics we play. We have to be quiet. We jump on a trampoline. We practice how to do pullovers.
> I love sports. If you don't play one, you should try one.

The power of organizing your thinking!

Children should have experiences writing their own informational text. As discussed throughout this chapter, they need time to read, sort, talk, and map before they write, so they can write from a place of conceptual understanding.

I encourage teachers to have children work in pairs or small groups in the beginning, as they need much talk and interaction to process the information for writing. Have them record facts they think are important as they read. Have them write each fact on a small strip of paper (cut an 8½" x 11" paper into six to eight strips) or index card. (It is okay if the partners end up writing similar or even identical facts.) Then, have them sort their facts into categories, just as Beth's students did in the scenario on pages 191–193.

Have them "organize and prioritize." Let children know that they do NOT have to use all the facts that they have written. Label the categories. Tell them writers sort and resort their information.

Kathy Hebert wanted to introduce her first graders to informational writing on their own. She wrote down the facts about ladybugs over the course of several days as she read

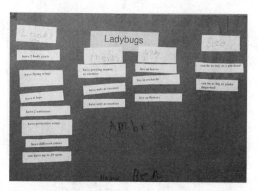

This is a first-grade sample of sorted facts from Kathy's class.

several different texts with her students. After collecting 20 to 30 facts, Kathy typed them on small sorting cards. She gave each group a set of cards. The students talked and sorted the cards into different piles and in different ways. Then they talked and labeled their categories with sticky notes. After the cards were sorted, Kathy asked each group to choose only two or three categories that they wanted to write about. They talked and made decisions. Then they created a hierarchical map by gluing their cards onto a piece of construction paper, with the categories at the top of the page. This was their map for writing their informational piece. By this point, these first graders were ready to write from a place of understanding.

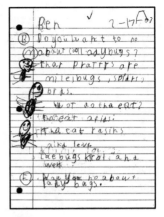

This is a first-grade sample of an organized piece of writing about ladybugs.

Tips for Writing Information Accurately and Creatively

→ Write your facts.

→ Sort the facts and label the categories.

→ Choose which categories to write about.

→ Talk to someone about what you will write.

→ Follow a GO map when writing.

Questions to Ask Yourself

→ How should the information be organized?

→ How can I add what I already know to my writing?

→ What kind of beginning will connect to the reader?

→ What can I say in the end to wrap things up for the reader?

→ What access features does my reader need to understand the information?

→ What connections or interpretations can I add?

→ Is my writing interesting to read?

Debbie Sterling's second graders did research in a similar fashion, only the students were able to write their own facts on strips of paper. They sorted to organize and prioritize. Each group came up with three categories that they would use to organize their informational text. They included a beginning and an end, as well as an access feature or a diagram. Each piece's organization and features were unique.

As Judy Hankel's second graders sorted and re-sorted their categories about inventions, new perspectives about the information emerged. Judy encouraged her students to choose the categories of information that they were most interested in to write about. Her students' writing no longer sounded flat and mechanical, one like the next, but instead took on personality and voice, reflecting their individual interests. Nathan wrote about inventors and what they invented; Abby compared inventions today to inventions long ago; Drew was intrigued with the creation of the Titanic and wrote specifically about that; and Hayley wrote about how to make an invention. These are information-literate primary students, able to "use information accurately and creatively" (Standard Three; see Chapter 1).

Edit for Organization

As children learn to organize information, incorporate editing and revising into the process. Teach students how to edit their writing, and at the same time reinforce the aspects of organization that you have been teaching. Teach students to look for specific organizing aspects in their writing: What is good about my writing? What am I doing well? What did I leave out that I can add? Having students look for their own successes is a powerful editing tool.

Identify two or three important criteria that children should include in their writing. Create a checklist for these criteria. Have students find each one in their writing and

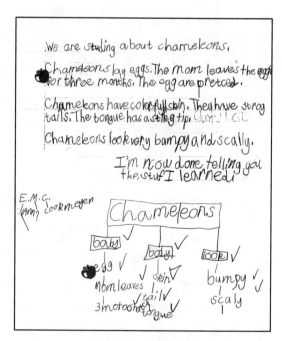

This is a child's sample of editing for organization: "Did I include the facts on my plan?"

Teaching the Information Generation

mark it with a sticker. Students can look for the following:

- The beginning
- The ending
- The key concepts from the map
- Details for each concept
- Signal words (for example, sequence words used with a sequential or cyclical map)

Students can also overlay the house onto their writing to determine the beginning, middle, and end. This is a visual for them to see if any part is missing.

Assessing Evaluating Text for Conceptual Understanding: Behaviors to Look for in Student Reading and Writing

As you assess the strategy, look for signs of conceptual understanding. Are students able to begin organizing their thinking? Do they look for connections within the text? Can they see the overall organizing pattern of the information? You can gain insight into your children's understanding by adapting familiar assessments to reflect how children are learning to evaluate for conceptual understanding: You can observe and listen to discussions, create checklists, and assess content learning.

Observe and Listen to Discussions

First grader Sean told his classmate Victor, "You can't use that map because you are talking about the life cycle, and order matters when you tell

Behaviors to Look and Listen For

(Behaviors that indicate students are organizing to learn the new information)

- Conversations during sorting
- Sharing thinking while sorting
- Asking: Does order matter?
- Talking through thinking about order
- Trying to find how information is connected
- Using more than one kind of GO map
- Knowing when to use each kind of GO map
- Talking and planning before writing
- Sharing how they decided about their GO map
- Looking for organization rather than just pulling out facts
- Being able to identify the beginning, middle, and end
- Anticipating the beginning, middle, and end
- Elaborating visuals and including the information in their mapping

about the life cycle." Victor respectfully explained his thinking, "Yes, I can. You see I am just saying that the ladybug has four stages. It is just a little fact. I am not explaining about the life cycle. I am listing facts about the ladybug. This is just one fact. So my map works."

These are two first graders well on their way to becoming conceptual thinkers and writers. As Beth listened and observed during writer's workshop, she knew this pair was organizing to learn. They were considering what kind of information to share about ladybugs and how that information needed to be organized.

As children work in pairs and groups to create maps and write information, listen to their conversations. Talk should be an integral part of the writing process. For talk not only reveals thinking, but helps students to think about the information and plan their writing. If they are talking about their writing, they are thinking and planning. As children are talking, listen for language that reflects this planning process.

Listen to and observe students during content area discussions, shared read-alouds, and guided reading groups. Conference with individual students during reader's workshop or guided reading groups to assess if they are organizing to learn as they read. You can use these questions during the conference to assess students' ability to begin organizing their thinking:

- Did the author include a beginning in this text? Can you show it to me?

- What connection is the author sharing with us? How did that help you to get ready to read the new information?

- Does order matter in this text? What makes you say that?

- How would you map this information?

- What visuals or access features helped you in understanding this section?

- Does this text include an ending? Can you show it to me?

- What did the author tell us in the end? Why do you think the author included that information?

- How can you tell me what this text is about with as few words as possible (summarize)?

Create Checklists

Create checklists that will include the strategy of organizing. These checklists can be used for sorting activities, mapping, or retelling. They can be used during content area reading, for guided reading, or with paired reading. They can be used for editing and revising writing. As you create these checklists, remember to focus on only three to five criteria

Teaching the Information Generation

and to make these criteria explicit to your students: What organizing behaviors do you want to see reflected in student thinking, language, reading, or writing?

Assess Content Learning

Since information-literate students are expected to multitask (thinking about the content, thinking about thinking, and thinking about the text), we also need to make sure that we multitask our assessment (assess thinking about the content, thinking about thinking, and thinking about the text). Retellings are a powerful way to multitask our assessment and assess all three kinds of thinking necessary for information literacy while assessing what students learned about the content. The checklist in the appendix, on page 217, can be used to assess thinking about information at the literal, critical, and conceptual level.

Retellings (both oral and written) reveal not only what the child understood but how they understood it as well (Benson & Cummins, 2000; Cambourne & Brown, 1987; Irwin & Mitchell, 1983). The retelling will reveal what students thought was important in the information. It will reveal their emerging ability to organize or expose their still-random thinking. Are they able to do the "between paragraph" thinking so critical to organizing? Retellings will give you insight into which readers are basic readers and which are moving toward proficiency.

For nonfiction retelling, and because we are assessing the strategy of organizing, all retellings should begin with a GO map. Children need to visually organize the information before they retell. You can begin assessing understanding of the information with a teacher-provided GO map in the beginning, and then move children toward creating their own GO map. This process alone will reveal insight into children's developing organizational strategies. As well, because children are learning how to retell as you are assessing their understanding, it is important that they read the text as many times as necessary to feel comfortable with the information and to be able to map the information (Cambourne & Brown, 1987). Once children have created the GO map, you can assess with the map itself, an oral retelling, or a written retelling.

Looking at students' GO maps can be part of the retelling assessment or even a viable alternative for assessment (Bromley et al., 1995). When there isn't time to allow students to retell, you can have them map the information and assess their work. I have learned that these graphic organizers reveal much about student thinking and conceptual understanding. Look to see if students were able to focus on key concepts within the text. Could they determine what was important? Did they pull out facts rather than looking to see how those facts were related? Look to see if the map matches the organization of the information.

Assessing With Nonfiction Retellings

As you listen to or read children's retellings, you can see how students are processing the information.

➜ Is there a literal level of thinking? A regurgitation of facts?

➜ Could the child tell the information in her own words?

➜ Did the child understand the content by seeing the relationship of ideas and facts?

➜ Did the child identify key concepts and supporting details?

➜ Does the retelling match the logical order of the information?

➜ Does the retelling reflect inferencing? Did the child add information not found directly in the text? Did she include the information in the visuals?

➜ Did the child make personal connections to the new information?

➜ How much teacher support was needed?

➜ Does the retelling reflect nonfiction strategies (making connections, elaborating visuals, recognizing headings, organizing information)?

The choice of map reveals a lot about their thinking and if they are able to determine importance in a text. For example, students in a first-grade class mapped the information about the life cycle of ladybugs after we read the text. When looking through their organizer maps, I found most all the children used a cyclical or sequential map to reflect the life cycle. However, Josiah used a concept map. The information around the concept map was isolated details (an insect hides in winter, chooses mate, is yellow, lays eggs, turns red). This gave me and his teacher the insight that this child had not yet learned how to organize and needed more assistance in organizing to learn.

When the map reflects a discrepancy with the information, I usually allow children the opportunity to explain or defend their map. Sometimes there is legitimate thinking behind why they chose the kind of map that they did. Asking them to explain also lets me know if they can put their thinking into words. Do they know why they made this decision, or did they just pull out a map and fill it in?

Closing Thoughts

Children learn to organize their thinking to learn new information. As they read, they know there is mental work that they must do. They know that while they read they must multitask. They must consider the following:

- Look for connections: *What is important here?*

- Connections lead to inferencing: *How is the information related?*

- Inferencing leads to organizing: *How can we organize the connections?*

- Organizing leads to visualizing: *How can we show the relationship?*

Learning how to organize is a powerful tool for evaluating text critically, competently, and conceptually so that readers have a framework for thinking about the information at a critical level of comprehension. It is not just providing structure for writing a text or paragraph, but developing options for thinking about reading and then providing choices for different ways to think about organizing information and sharing it with others.

CHAPTER 8

Transforming Classroom Practice:

Lessons From the Field

To this point, I have written this book with your students in mind. Chapters 1 and 2 laid the foundation for understanding the role of information literacy in today's world for today's Information Generation students. The strategy chapters provided concrete tools for teaching primary students how to become information literate: to access, evaluate, and use information at literal, critical, and conceptual levels of understanding. Each chapter provided ways to help students learn. This chapter is designed to help *you* learn, as you embark on your own professional journey. To get the most out of the journey, you must be open to changing the way you teach. Perhaps teaching informational text will require a change in teaching literacy or in teaching content areas. Maybe teaching critical and conceptual thinking will require a change in how you plan and develop lessons and interact with students. Or learning to dialogue with children will require a change to your classroom environment. Changes like these can be difficult, but they're worth the struggle because they can lead to deeper learning and more satisfying teaching.

As a veteran teacher who has worked with the strategies described in this book for over a decade, and who has worked with teachers in transition over the past two decades, I wrote this last chapter to help you make the most of the journey. To get started, allow me to share a *personal* story of change.

Not too long ago, I married an incredible guy, John—my long-awaited life partner. "Love the second time around," as the singer crooned at our wedding, since I had been down the aisle once before. Being married again after being single for eight years was an exciting change for me. However, I wasn't prepared for change as a journey. *And it caught me by surprise.* Ironically, as a professional staff developer, I am often considered a "change agent"—an expert in facilitating change. Yet when faced with change myself, I struggled. I had not prepared myself for the *process* of change—the transition from the "old me" to the "new me."

In the beginning I struggled. For starters, I hyphenated my last name, Benson-Castagna. However, I soon began realizing there were problems with this. First, airlines cannot hyphenate names on their computers, so my name appeared as Vicki Bensoncastagna on tickets. (The airline agent asked me to please pronounce my name, as that was the most unusual name he had ever seen!) And when I changed my state-issued picture ID, which is required to travel, the Department of Public Safety couldn't fit all the letters in the space provided. So Benson became my middle name and Castagna my last. That was okay by me . . . until an airline representative told me I didn't have a reservation. Turns out that Benson-Castagna is listed under the B's in the system, while she was looking for Castagna. After much searching and explaining, she found the reservation. Then airport security insisted I couldn't fly because my ID didn't match the hard-earned, much-discussed ticket! From there, the rental-car agent informed me that the name on my credit card, Benson-Castagna, was not the same name on the driver's license and, therefore, denied me a car. And you can only imagine when a school system booked my airline ticket for the next trip as Vicki Benson what complications and difficulties arose!

In the end I chose "Benson Castagna" (no hyphen), but more important, I realized that there was a lot more to this than a name change. My trials and tribulations at the airport reminded me that I was on more than one kind of journey. Not only was I transitioning from home to my consulting job, but also from the old me to the new me.

So I take this opportunity to share some lessons about the process of change—drawing parallels from my *personal change* to help you with your *professional change*. By paying attention to the process of change and being aware of what to expect, you can embrace the process rather than struggle through it.

Lesson #1: Change Requires Change

This is a profound lesson if there ever was one—and one that we tend to overlook. Even when change is good and desirable, it alters our time, our energy, and our life. Life as it was, no longer is. And that can be discomforting. Getting remarried was definitely something that I wanted, wished for, looked forward to. But in making this decision, I had to shift my thinking about life. Rethink what it looked like, what it *could* look like, and how it would be different. Decisions had to be made. I lived in Louisiana, John in Texas. We both have careers that require a lot of national and international travel. I have three children. John has four. I have a house and two dogs, John has a house and one dog. Getting married required *changing life as we each knew it.*

When it comes to educating primary students, you are inspired and motivated to teach information literacy. You have made a decision to help this Information Generation

After creating a GO! Chart with students, Debbie Sterling listens in on small groups sharing their connections.

learn to think using informational text. You can see how cognitive strategies might better prepare them for those state and national tests. You want to try out the Go! Chart. However, let me put you on alert: *Change requires change.* To implement the ideas in this book, a shift must occur. Decisions will have to be made. In order to embrace the new, you must rethink how to spend your time, where to focus your energy, and how you will redefine your role as teacher.

But what if change is not your choice? Isn't that how it often works in education? Change originates from another source, such as the principal's office, the district, the state, or the federal government. It could even be brought about by the technological age in which we live and the Information Generation of kids that we teach.

All of a sudden these changes are impacting our classroom decisions. Someone else's demands are impacting our lives, and we find ourselves asking questions about using "my time" to do "their required stuff." Where do we find time for this new curriculum? How do we meet all the new guidelines? How do they expect us to get this all done? How will I find time to add one more thing to an already full day? And we lament, "Our classrooms will never be the same ever again anymore!"

What's the best way to cope with enforced change? As one teacher so appropriately remarked, "If change is so good, then you go first." She was wise enough to know that change would require change in her classroom. And that is the first step: Expect change. Look ahead and visualize where you want to go. *What might my classroom look like with cognitive strategies for informational text? Where does this fit into my curriculum and my day? How will my schedule be impacted? What new resources will this require?* See children talking through the text in whole groups, small groups, and with partners. See them excited about learning from informational text, creating their own graphic organizers.

Stephen R. Covey (2004), a leadership guru and author of the best-selling *The 7 Habits of Highly Effective People,* calls this "beginning with the end in mind." Effective people know where they are going. Look ahead and visualize where you want to go.

Teaching the Information Generation

Tips for a Smooth Transition to Teaching Information Literacy

→ Visit with another teacher who uses informational text well and is skilled at teaching literal, critical, and conceptual thinking. See what it looks like in his classroom. What does dialogue sound like?

→ Look for lesson plans on the Internet or in books. How can you use them to help teach students to predict, use access features, read for literal understanding, make connections and interpretations, or organize information?

→ Take a moment to reflect on what your classroom might look like down the road. What do you see? Write down your intentions for teaching information literacy. Think through how to take your current resources and schedule and adapt the strategies to your present situation. You have taken the first step on the journey toward successful change.

→ Do more reading about strategy instruction and nonfiction. Consider what other teachers and educators have done and discovered. Here are some resources that I've found useful:

Graphic Organizers: Visual Strategies for Active Learning, by Karen Bromley, Linda Irwin-DeVitis, and Marcia Modlo (Scholastic)

Non-fiction Writing Strategies: Using Science Big Books as Models, by Marcia Freeman (Maupin House)

Starting with Comprehension: Reading Strategies for the Youngest Learners, by Andie Cunningham and Ruth Shagoury (Stenhouse)

Teaching Reading in Social Studies, Science, and Math, by Laura Robb (Scholastic)

Teaching Students to Read Nonfiction: Grades 2–4, by Alice Boynton and Wiley Blevins (Scholastic)

Lesson # 2: Change Requires Relationships

Michael Fullan (2001), an expert in leading change, asserts that building relationships is one of the most important routes to effective change. As he puts it, "Effective change is all about relationships, relationships, relationships." Relationships are especially important when the change doesn't originate from you but impacts you. This has certainly been true in my family. John and I had to listen to our children's responses and their fears about all the change that we created; we needed to allow our children to get frustrations out in the open, to not let those unspoken fears sit and fester. We tried to anticipate how we would handle the new, the unknown. We asked, "What *might* Christmas begin to look like?" It was important to spend much time nurturing these relationships. It was imperative to the success of our own change.

Kathy Herbert offers feedback about using a nonfiction strategy.

And so it is with professional change. Peter Senge, author of *Schools That Learn* (2000), contends that to negotiate school change, we must provide relationship-building opportunities for faculty. Teachers need to be able to express their concerns and fears about change. Teachers need to talk through how unknowns will impact their classrooms, their time, their energy, and themselves. They must move beyond their personal concerns so they can deal with how the change will affect students and learning. By talking through personal concerns, teachers are more likely to better understand and accept change.

As you travel on your professional journey, bring along fellow travelers. Seek out and create a support group with other teachers. Explore how new changes might look, in practical, constructive ways. Brainstorm resources. Work together to plan. Share your concerns and celebrate your successes.

Create a group and discuss the chapters and strategies in this book. Try out a lesson and get feedback from another group member. Talk about what worked and what didn't. Return to the text for support. And talk more. In my own research and work with teachers, collegial support was a key factor in the success, or lack thereof, of strategy implementation.

The first step toward change is recognizing that it requires change—whether we have initiated it or not. The second is to cultivate relationships to help us work through issues associated with change.

Teaching the Information Generation

Lesson #3: Change Requires Letting Go

To embrace something new, we must let something go. William Bridges (1980, 2001, 2003), author of many books on change, says that a lot of people aren't successful with change because they haven't acknowledged—and even grieved over—what they are leaving behind in order to embrace the new change.

I found myself going through this process as I was packing up my house in Louisiana for my move to Texas. Over the past years life has taken me many places, through many phases of children's lives, and on many adventures. I had collected quite a houseful. However I began realizing that I simply couldn't take everything. If John and I both moved everything we had from our separate houses to our new house, we wouldn't be able to fit it all. And even if we could fit it, would we need it? After all, what would we do with a combined total of 26 Corningware dishes? I began evaluating as I was packing: *What purpose in my life did this serve? Was it appropriate for that time only, or would it move us forward?* And, upon answering questions like those, I found myself letting go and, in the process, grieving the loss of some things. But I let go in order to embrace the new.

As you begin to try out new strategies, be fearless about casting off what isn't working to make room for them. Take a hard look at your schedule, your library, your lesson plans, your assessment tools—everything. This process is necessary for effective change. Evaluate your present situation in light of where you are and where you want to be.

Brandi Appe guides her kindergarteners in talking about the order of information, using the take-apart-and-chart activity.

Too often we teachers have our "sacred cows." You know, those things that we hold onto just because we hold onto them. Or that are comfortable. Or that simply always have been that way. Consider the following:

- Do you need to let go of the notion that a "quiet classroom is a good classroom" in order to embrace the fact that children need to talk to learn? Grieve letting go of that silence.

- Are the questions in the teacher's guide for science and social studies comforting? If so, acknowledge that, but then listen to student responses and trust yourself to guide thinking and conversations.

♦ Is letting go of worksheets hard? Do you need to let go of expecting "one correct answer" to move toward myriad answers that result from interpretations, connections, and critical thinking?

Take a close look at your classroom, your materials, your time, your routines, your activities, your expectations, and the strategies you are using. Hold each one up to examination. *What purpose does this serve? Will it move my students forward to where we need to go?* Then make a list of those that you think you might need to relinquish.

And don't forget to give yourself permission to grieve them, turning to those collegial relationships for support and understanding. Talk through the feelings of letting go, knowing that it is part of the change process. This will help you get to the "new" more smoothly and quickly. It is part of the journey.

Lesson #4: Change Requires Transition Time

"It isn't the change that will kill you," William Bridges (2003) says. "It's the *transition*." And just what is the transition? The place in between the old and the new.

For many teachers, this transitional period is a frustrating place. The old doesn't really work anymore, and the new isn't quite yet working. No man's land. This transition period has an impact on the success—or failure—of the change process.

After change has been introduced, people are aware of it, but they haven't acquired the skills and behaviors that the change requires. This time in between leaving the old and embracing the new is what Bridges calls "the Neutral Zone" (2003). He compares a person in transition to a trapeze artist letting go of one trapeze and being suspended in midair for those few seconds before grabbing on to the next one. No wonder change feels so uncomfortable!

You are an accomplished teacher, confident in what you have been doing over the years. Revising your practice requires, in a sense, going back to "square one." It requires leaving what you know for something far more tenuous. Life doesn't look the same anymore. It isn't comfortable. You're in the Neutral Zone.

Transition takes time. The Neutral Zone is inevitable. So many teachers find that the initial excitement they feel often fades when confronted with the realities of the classroom.

So what do we do? Follow the old proverb "The longest journey begins with the first step." Take that first step followed by a series of others until you've reached your planned outcome. Scaffold your own learning as you scaffold student learning. Rome wasn't built in a day, and neither should a better, more effective literacy program be. Transition takes time. Give this gift to yourself. Don't try to transform your teaching the first week of school!

Chapters 4 through 7 can be used as scaffolds. You can use them individually to support what you're trying to accomplish with students. For example, you can teach students the strategy of predicting (Chapter 4), applying only the ideas in that chapter initially. Weave the ideas into individual content areas. You might choose to introduce predicting to the whole class during science. Once you are comfortable with this strategy, then you can focus on guiding students in learning how to use the access features to create literal understanding (Chapter 5). Build each strategy onto the previous learning. Move into more critical and conceptual thinking (chapters 6 and 7) when you are comfortable with dialogue and informational text.

Be aware of the Neutral Zone and expect it. Remind yourself that discomfort is a natural part of being there and, thankfully, temporary. "This, too, shall pass." You are on the way.

Lesson #5: Change Requires Time

I could not believe that it had been months since our move to the new house and we were still in boxes—a couple hundred of them—filling our garage, spare bedrooms, and every other spare space. Walls needed pictures. Windows needed curtains. Change takes time. According to Bridges (1980), change must occur both externally and internally. In fact, several months after we were married, John introduced me as "My wife, Vicki Benson." Did he forget that we were married?! In reality, it took time for him to say "Vicki Castagna" naturally and automatically. The outward changes had taken place—the wedding, the marriage, the move. It took longer for the new to become the norm.

Developing a plan for writing is an expected routine in Beth Laine's first-grade classroom.

It takes time to make the change truly yours. You may make outward changes in your curriculum, schedule, and instruction; adjust your teaching to include more informational text; teach cognitive strategies; try out some of the writing ideas. However, it takes time for those outward changes to feel comfortable and become routine.

You may feel that you are having to think so hard about the procedure you are learning (*What do I do next?*) that you cannot listen to student responses. This is the transition time Bridges is talking about. You are still in the Neutral Zone. Teach cognitive strategies systematically so they become internal, the norm. Simply introducing them and using them every now and then only creates external change. Consistent use of the Go! Chart can help you avoid that. And when the instructional procedures are routine, you will be focused on supporting student learning. The external will have become internal.

A word to the wise: If, after a few weeks, you find these new routines aren't working, *adjust*. Step back and consider what is happening. Ask a colleague to observe and give feedback. Consider if your students need more support or less scaffolding. Do they need to be working with partners? Do you need to transfer the strategies to small groups? Are they ready to record their thinking with a journal or sticky notes as they read? Adjust until you find what works in your classroom with your set of students in your school. Then when you find that niche, stabilize and make it routine. Internalize the change.

We must allow ourselves that time for internalizing change for it to feel natural. We need to allow patience with our own learning. I have a reminder of this hanging in my office that says, "Have patience with all things. But first of all with yourself." We give our students support as they learn something new. We must also give it to ourselves.

Whether we initiate the change or somebody else does, we need to allow ourselves to try out new skills externally, knowing that the more comfortable we become with them, the more likely they are to transition internally. Until one day, we realize that we are out of the Neutral Zone, and the new change doesn't seem so new anymore. It is now the norm. And we couldn't imagine it any other way.

Closing Thoughts

Let me add a postscript to all this. As you work to create information-literate students, remember to keep your eyes on the big picture. Keep focused on the goal. It would be easy to get bogged down in the details of change. For my personal change, that meant focusing on my new life. Nurturing the relationships in this new blended family rather than focusing on the complex travel schedules, the boxes waiting to be unpacked, those airline security issues, the innumerable documents that needed name changes, publishing deadlines, juggling seven children's different high school, college, grad school, or work schedules in four different states . . . and on and on. Instead, we chose to embrace the journey. To not lose sight of the goal.

In the same way, don't lose sight of the goal professionally. It would be easy to get bogged down in the details of all this change. To focus on the frustrations and struggles of the Neutral Zone. To be overwhelmed with district expectations while juggling the new teaching strategies or to focus on the schedule changes, the resources required, or the logistics. Michael Fullan (1993) reminds us to always keep our moral purpose as our compass for our journey—our moral purpose being to prepare our students to be successful citizens. To keep in mind that the reason we seek change in our classroom is for our children. Because we know that in today's world our children must be information literate. We know we must help our young Information Generation students to:

- Access information efficiently and effectively

- Evaluate information critically and competently

- Use information accurately and creatively

We must help them to become information literate in today's classroom for tomorrow's world.

Keep in mind, the journey is all about the children. The reason we do what we do is for the kids. May we never lose sight of that.

Remember that the longest journey begins with the first step. And that you have taken. You are well on your way to teaching this Information Generation to become information literate.

Learning Log

Title: _____   Name: _____

Predictions	Vocabulary	Understanding
What kind of information might we learn . . .	I think the author might use these words . . .	I noticed these facts/attributes . . .

Learning Log

Title: _____   Name: _____

Interpretations	Connections	Organizing
I think . . . . I feel . . . . I wonder . . .	This is like	How will I organize this information?

Ways to Organize Information

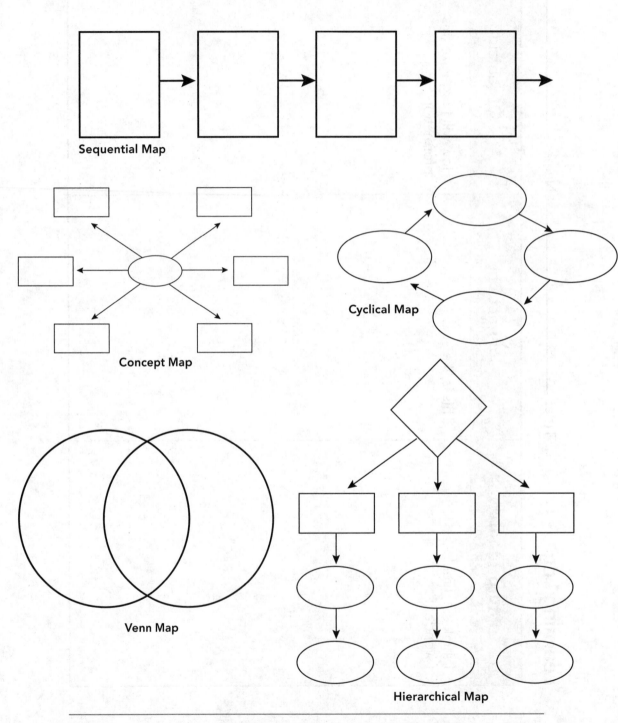

Sequential Map

Concept Map

Cyclical Map

Venn Map

Hierarchical Map

Teaching the Information Generation © 2007 Scholastic Professional

Retelling Information Rubric

	LITERAL UNDERSTANDING	CRITICAL UNDERSTANDING	CONCEPTUAL UNDERSTANDING
Advanced 4	Includes important concepts from the text in student's own words; incorporates access features in retelling; includes details and key technical vocabulary; demonstrates understanding of content	Infers beyond facts to interpret the information, and supports with facts from text; may give opinion and support from text; uses personal and other connections to discuss the content	Organizes information using appropriate graphic organizer (concept, hierarchical, sequential, cyclical, or Venn); matches retelling to organization of graphic organizer; can summarize the gist of the information
Proficient 3	Includes important concepts from the text in student's own words; incorporates access features in retelling; includes details and some key vocabulary; demonstrates understanding of content	Attempts to interpret information; connects information to life experiences; may attempt to make parallel connections	Organizes information using appropriate graphic organizer (concept, hierarchical, sequential, cyclical, or Venn); matches retelling to organization of graphic organizer; can summarize the gist of the information
Emerging 2	Includes some of the main concepts and details, mostly a list of facts; has difficulty putting the information into own words, often restating information in author's words; attempts to use access features with prompting	May relate text to own life in a peripheral way; attempts connections but unable to relate back to information; makes few or no interpretations	Attempts to organize information, but may not match information; may be able to retell when provided with a completed graphic organizer
Struggling 1	Includes random facts; may include irrelevant information or inaccuracies; copies or memorizes information; practices incomplete retelling	Makes no attempt to connect information to own life, even with prompting	Makes no attempt to organize the information

Professional References Cited

The American heritage dictionary of the English language (4th ed.). (2004). New York: Houghton Mifflin.

Beck, I. L., & McKeown, M. G. (2001). Text talk: Capturing the benefits of read-aloud experiences for young children. *The Reading Teacher, 55*(1), 10–20.

Beck, I. L., McKeown, M. G., & Kucan, L. (2002). *Bringing words to life: Robust vocabulary instruction.* New York: Guilford Press.

Benson, V., & Cummins, C. (2000). *The power of retelling.* Bothell, WA: Wright Group.

Bloom, B. S. (1984). *Taxonomy of educational objectives.* Boston, MA: Allyn & Bacon

Boynton, A., & Blevins, W. (2004). *Teaching students to read nonfiction: Grades 2–4.* New York: Scholastic.

Bransford, J. D., Brown, A. L., & Cocking, R. (Eds.). (2000). *How people learn: Brain, mind, experience, and school.* Washington, DC: National Academies Press.

Bransford, J. D., Stein, B. S., Shelton, T. S., & Owings, R. A. (1981). Cognition and adaption: The importance of learning to learn. In J. Harvey (Ed.), *Cognition, social behavior and environment.* Hillsdale, NJ: Erlbaum.

Braunger, J., & Lewis, J. (1997). *Building a knowledge base in reading.* Portland, OR: Northwest Regional Educational Laboratory's Curriculum and Instruction Services.

Bridges, W. (1980). *Transitions: Making sense of life's changes.* New York: Perseus.

Bridges, W. (2001). *The way of transition: Embracing life's most difficult moments.* New York: Perseus.

Bridges, W. (2003). *Managing transitions: Making the most of change.* New York: Perseus.

Bromley, K., Irwin-DeVitis, L., & Modlo, M. (1995). *Graphic organizers: Visual strategies for active learning.* New York: Scholastic.

Caine, R. N., & Caine, G. (1991). *Making connections: Teaching and the human brain.* Alexandria, VA: ASCD.

Calkins, L. (1994). *The art of teaching writing.* Portsmouth, NH: Heinemann.

Cambourne, B., & Brown, H. (1987). *Read and retell.* Portsmouth, NH: Heinemann.

Carrell, P. L. (1992). Awareness of text structure: Effects on recall. *Language Learning, 42*, 1–20.

Chall, J., Jacobs, V., & Baldwin, L. (1996). Reading, writing, and language connection. In J. Shimron (Ed.), *Literacy and education: Essays in memory of Dina Feitelson* (pp. 33–48). Cresskill, NJ: Hampton Press.

Chomsky, C. (1972). Stages in language development and reading exposure. *Harvard Educational Review, 42*(1), 1–33.

Costa, A. L. (1991). *The school as a home for the mind.* Arlington Heights, IL: Skylight.

Covey, S. (2004). *The 7 habits of highly effective people.* New York: Simon and Schuster.

Cuban, L. (1993). *How teachers taught: Constancy and change in American classrooms 1890–1990.* New York: Teachers College Press.

Cunningham, A., & Shagoury, R. (2005). *Starting with comprehension: Reading strategies for the youngest learners.* Portland, ME: Stenhouse.

Daniels, H., & Zemelman, S. (2004). *Subjects matter: Every teacher's guide to content-area reading.* Portsmouth, NH: Heinemann.

Dorn, L., & Soffos, C. (2005). *Teaching for deep comprehension: A reading workshop approach.* Portland, ME: Stenhouse.

Doyle, C. (1996). Information literacy: Status report from the United States. In D. Booker (Ed.), *Learning for life: Information literacy and the autonomous learner* (pp. 39-48). Adelaide, South Australia: University of South Australia.

Dreher, M. J. (2003). Motivating struggling readers by tapping the potential of information books. *Reading & Writing Quarterly, 19*, 25–38.

Duffy, G. G. (1993). Rethinking strategy instruction: Four teachers' development and their low achievers' understandings. *Elementary School Journal, 93*(3), 231–247.

Duffy, G. G. (2002). The case for direct explanation of strategies. In C. C. Block & M. Pressley (Eds.), *Comprehension instruction: Research-based best practices.* New York: Guilford Press.

Duke, N. (2000). 3.6 minutes per day: The scarcity of informational text in first grade. *Reading Research Quarterly, 35*(2), 202–224.

Duke, N., & Bennett-Armistead, V. S. (2003). *Reading & writing informational text in the primary grades: Research-based practices* New York: Scholastic.

Duke, N., & Kays, J. (1998). "Can I say 'Once upon a time'?": Kindergarten children developing knowledge of information book language. *Early Childhood Research Quarterly, 13*(2), 295–318.

Elder, L., & Paul, R. (2003). *The foundations of analytical thinking: How to take thinking apart and what to look for when you do.* Dillon Beach, CA: The Foundation for Critical Thinking.

Ellis, E. (1997). Watering-up instruction for adolescents with mild disabilities: The knowledge dimension. *Remedial and Special Education, 18*, 326–346.

Ellis, E. (2004). Makes sense strategies model. Retrieved September 20, 2004, from http://www.graphicorganizers.com/Sara/ArticlesAbout/MSS%20rationale.doc

Facione, P. A. (2006). Critical thinking: What it is and why it counts [electronic version]. *Insight Assessment*. Retrieved June 22, 2006, from http://insightassessment.com/articles.html

Fisher, C. W., & Hiebert, E. H. (1990). Characteristics of tasks in two approaches to literature instruction. *Elementary School Journal, 91*, 3–18.

Freeman, M. (2000). *Non-fiction writing strategies: Using science big books as models*. Gainesville, FL: Maupin House.

Freeman, M. (2003a). *Building a writing community: A practical guide*. Gainesville, FL: Maupin House.

Freeman, M. (2003b). Using writing to assess student understanding of informational text. *The NERA Journal, 39*(1), 21–28.

Fullan, M. (1993). *Change force: Probing the depths of educational reform*. New York: The Falmer Press.

Fullan, M. (2001). *Leading in a culture of change*. San Francisco: Jossey-Bass.

Galda, L., Cullinan, B. E., & Strickland, D. S. (1993). *Language, literacy and the child* (2nd ed.). New York: Harcourt Brace College Publishers.

Glaser, R. (1989). Expertise and learning: How do we think about instructional processes now that we have discovered knowledge structure? In D. Klahr & K. Kotosky (Eds.), *Complex information processing: The impact of Herbert A. Simon* (pp. 269–282). Hillsdale, NJ: Erlbaum.

Gordon, C. J., & Pearson, P. D. (1983). *The effects of instruction on metacomprehension and inferencing on children's comprehension abilities* (Tech. Report No. 227). Urbana: University of Illinois, Center for the Study of Reading.

Graesser, A. C., & Person, N. K. (1994). Question asking during tutoring. *American Educational Research Journal, 31*, 104–107.

Graves, D. (1994). *A fresh look at writing*. Portsmouth, NH: Heinemann.

Hallowell, E. M. (2006). *Crazybusy: Overstretched, overbooked, and about to snap! Strategies for coping in a world gone ADD*. New York: Ballantine Books.

Hammer, M. (1997). *Beyond reengineering: How the process-centered organization is changing our work and lives*. New York: HarperCollins.

Hansen, J. (1981). The effects of inference training and practice on young children's reading comprehension. *Reading Research Quarterly, 16*, 391–417.

Harris, T., & Hodges, R. (Eds.). (1995). *The literacy dictionary: The vocabulary of reading and writing*. Newark, DE: International Reading Association.

Hartman, D. K. (1994). The intertextual links of readers using multiple passages: A postmodern/semiotic/cognitive view of meaning making. In R. B. Ruddell, M. R. Ruddell, & H. Singer (Eds.), *Theoretical models and processes of reading* (pp. 616–636). Newark, DE: International Reading Association.

Harvey, S. (1998). *Nonfiction matters: Reading, writing, and research in grades 3–8*. Portland, ME: Stenhouse.

Harvey, S., & Goudvis, A. (2000). *Strategies that work: Teaching comprehension to enhance understanding*. York, Maine: Stenhouse.

Henjy, M. (2004). Understanding students, understanding mathematics. *Thinking Classroom, 5*(2), 13–19.

Hoffman, J. V., McCarthey, S. J., Christian, C., Corman, L., Dressman, M., Elliott, B., et al. (1994). So what's new in the new basals? A focus on first grade. *Journal of Reading Behavior, 26*, 47–73.

Hoffman, J. V., Roser, N. L., & Battle, J. (1993). Reading aloud in classrooms: From modal to a "model." *The Reading Teacher, 46*, 496–505.

Hyerle, D. (1996). *Visual tools for constructing knowledge*. Alexandria, VA: ASCD.

Information literacy standards for student learning. (1998). Chicago: American Association of School Librarians and Association for Educational Communications and Technology.

Irwin, P. A., & Mitchell, J. N. (1983). A procedure for assessing the richness of retellings. *Journal of Reading, 26*, 391–396.

Jones, B. F., Palinscar, A. S., Ogle, D., & Carr, E. G. (Eds.). (1987). *Strategic teaching and learning: Cognitive instruction in the content areas*. Alexandria, VA: Association of Supervision and Curriculum Development.

Kamil, M. L., & Lane, D. (1997). Using information text for first grade reading instruction: Theory and practice. Retrieved June 17, 2000, from http://www.stanford.edu/~mkamil/nrc97b.htm

Keene, E. O., & Zimmerman, S. (1997). *Mosaic of thought: Teaching comprehension in a reader's workshop*. Portsmouth, N.H.: Heinemann.

Kerry, S. (2002). Memory and retention time. Retrieved July 16, 2003, from http://www.education-reform.net/memory.htm

Keys, C. W. (1999). Revitalizing instruction in scientific genres: Connecting knowledge production with writing to learn in science. *Science Education, 83*, 115–130.

Kintsch, W. (1987). Contributions from cognitive psychology. In P. L. Anders, J. N. Mitchell, & R. J. Tierney (Eds.), *Understanding readers' understanding: Theory and practice*. Hillsdale, NJ: Erlbaum.

Kintsch, W. (1994). The role of knowledge in discourse processing: A construction-integration model. In R. B. Ruddell, M. R. Ruddell, & H. Singer (Eds.), *Theoretical models and processes of reading* (pp. 951–995). Newark, DE: International Reading Association.

Kintsch, W. (1998). *Comprehension: A paradigm for cognition*. New York: Cambridge University Press.

Kintsch, W., & van Dijk, T. A. (1978). Toward a model of text comprehension and production. *Psychological Review, 85*, 363–394.

Lapp, D., Flood, J., & Farnan, N. (1996). *Content area reading and learning: Instructional strategies*. Boston: Allyn & Bacon.

Loftus, G. R., & Loftus, E. F. (1976). *Human memory: The processing of information*. Hillsdale, NJ: Erlbaum.

Macken-Horarik, M. (2002). Something to shoot for: A systematic functional approach to teaching genre in secondary school science. In A. M. Johns (Ed.), *Genre in the classroom: Multiple perspectives* (pp. 17–42). Mahwah, NJ: Erlbaum.

McGee, L. M., & Richgels, D. J. (1982). Text structure strategies. In E. K. Dishner, T. W. Bean, J. E. Readence, & D. W. Moore (Eds.), *Reading in the content areas: Improving classroom instruction* (3rd ed., pp. 234–245). Dubuque, IA: Kendall/Hunt.

McKenzie, J. (1996). Making web meaning. *Educational Leadership, 54*, 30–32.

McPherson, F. (2000). *The memory key*. New York: Career Press.

Miller, G. A. (1956). The magical number seven, plus or minus two: Some limits on our capacity for processing information. *Psychological Review, 63*, 81–97.

Moline, S. (1995). *I see what you mean: Children at work with visual information*. New York: Stenhouse.

Mooney, M. (2003). Thinking as a reader and writer of informational text. In L. Hoyt, M. Mooney, & B. Parkes (Eds.), *Exploring informational texts: From theory to practice* (pp. 8–17). Portsmouth, NH: Heinemann.

Moss, B. (1993). *Using retellings to assess children's comprehension of expository text*. Paper presented at the National Reading Conference, Charleston, SC.

Myers, M. (1996). *Changing our mind: Negotiating English and literacy*. Urbana, IL: National Council of Teachers of English.

National assessment of educational progress: The nation's report card: Reading 2005. (2005). Washington, DC: National Center for Educational Statistics.

The neglected "R": The need for a writing revolution. (2003). National Commission on Writing in America's Schools and Colleges.

Newkirk, T. (1989). *More than stories: The range of children's writing*. Portsmouth, NH: Heinemann.

Osborne, R., & Wittrock, M. (1983). Learning science: A generative process. *Science Education, 67*, 289–508.

Palinscar, A. S., & Brown, A. L. (1984). Reciprocal teaching of comprehension-fostering and comprehension-monitoring activities. *Cognition and Instruction, 1*(2), 117–175.

Pappas, C. C. (2006). The information book genre: Its role in integrated science literacy research and practice. *Reading Research Quarterly, 41*(2), 226–250.

Pearson, P. D. (1993). Teaching and learning reading: A research perspective. *Language Arts, 70*, 502–511.

Pearson, P. D., & Fielding, L. (1991). Comprehension instruction. In R. Barr, M. Kamil, P. Mosenthal, & P. D. Pearson (Eds.), *Handbook of reading research* (vol. 2, pp. 815–860). New York: Longman.

Pearson, P. D., Roehler, L. R., Dole, J. A., & Duffy, G. G. (1992). Developing expertise in reading comprehension. In S. J. Samuels & A. E. Farstrup (Eds.), *What research has to say about reading instruction* (2nd ed., pp. 145–199). Newark, DE: International Reading Association.

Perrone, V. (1994). How to engage students in learning. *Educational Leadership, 51*, 11–13.

Prensky, M. (2001a). Digital native, digital immigrants. *On the Horizon, 9*(5), 1–6.

Prensky, M. (2001b). Do they really think differently? *On the Horizon, 9*(6), 1–7.

Prensky, M. (2006). *"Don't bother me Mom—I'm learning."* New York: Paragon Publishing House.

Presidential committee report on information literacy. (1989). Retrieved February 3, 2002, from http://www.infolit.org/documents/89Report.htm

Pressley, M. (2002). Comprehension strategies instruction: A turn-of-the-century status report. In C. C. Block & M. Pressley (Eds.), *Comprehension instruction: Research-based best practices.* New York: Guilford Press.

Pressley, M., & El-Dinary, P. B. (1992). Memory strategy instruction that promotes good information processing. In D. Herrman, H. Weingartner, A. Searleman, & C. McEvoy (Eds.), *Memory improvement: Implications for memory theory.* New York: Springer-Verlag.

Pressley, M., Johnson, C. J., Symons, S., McGold-rick, J. A., & Kurita, J. A. (1989). Strategies that improve children's memory and comprehension of text. *Elementary School Journal, 90*(1), 3–32.

Pressley, M., & Woloshyn, V. (1995). *Cognitive strategy instruction that really improves children's academic performance.* Cambridge, MA: Brookline Books.

Pressley, M., Wood, E., Woloshyn, V., Martin, V., King, A., & Menke, D. (1992). Encouraging mindful use of prior knowledge: Attempting to construct explanatory answers facilitates learning. *Educational Psychologist, 27,* 91–110.

Reading for understanding: Toward an R&D program in reading comprehension. (2002). Santa Monica, CA; Washington, DC: RAND Education.

Reading framework for the 2003 national assessment of educational progress. (2003). Washington, DC: National Assessment of Educational Progress.

Report of the National Reading Panel: Teaching children to read: An evidence-based assessment of the scientific research literature on reading and its implications for reading instruction. (2000). Washington, DC: National Institute of Child Health and Human Development, National Institutes of Health.

Robb, L. (1999). *Reading strategies that work.* New York: Scholastic.

Robb, L. (2003). *Teaching reading in social studies, science, and math.* New York: Scholastic.

Roberts, D. F., Foehr, U. G., Rideout, V. J., & Brodie, M. (2005). *Generation M: Media in the lives of 8-18 year-olds.* Washington, DC: Kaiser Family Foundation.

Rosenblatt, L. M. (1994). The transactional theory of reading and writing. In R. B. Ruddell, M. R. Ruddell, & H. Singer (Eds.), *Theoretical models and processes of reading* (4th ed., pp. 1057–1092). Newark, DE: International Reading Association.

Rosenhine, B., Meier, D., & Chapman, S. (1996). Teaching students to generate questions: A review of the intervention studies. *Review of Educational Research, 66*(2), 181–122.

Rosenhine, B., & Meister, C. (1994). Reciprocal teaching: A review of the research. *Review of Educational Research, 64*(4), 479–530.

Rothery, J. (1996). Making changes: Developing an educational linguistics. In R. G. W. Hasan (Ed.), *Literacy in society* (pp. 86–123). New York: Longman.

Routman, R. (2003). *Reading essentials.* Portsmouth, NH: Heinemann.

Senge, P., Cambron-McCabe, N., Lucas, T., Smith, B., Dutton, J., & Kleiner, A. (2000). *Schools that learn: A fifth discipline fieldbook for educators, parents, and everyone who cares about education.* New York: Doubleday.

Smith, F. (1990). *To think.* New York: Teachers College Press.

Spiro, R., & Taylor, B. M. (1987). On investigating children's transition from narrative to expository discourse: The multidimensional nature of psychological text classification. In R. J. Tierney, P. L. Anders, & J. N. Mitchell (Eds.), *Understanding readers' understanding* (pp. 77–93). Hillsdale, NJ: Erlbaum.

Stead, T. (2005). *Reality checks: Teaching reading comprehension with nonfiction, K–5.* Portland, ME: Stenhouse.

Strickland, D. S., & Morrow, L. M. (Eds.). (1989). *Emerging literacy: Young children learn to read and write.* Newark, DE: International Reading Association.

Suid, M., & Lincoln, W. (1988). *Recipes for writing: Motivation, skills, and activities.* New York: Addison Wesley.

Tapscott, D. (1999). *Growing up digital: The rise of the net generation.* New York: McGraw-Hill.

Taylor, B. M. (1992). Text structure, comprehension, and recall. In S. J. Samuels & A. E. Farstrup (Eds.), *What research has to say about reading instruction* (pp. 220–235). Newark, DE: International Reading Association.

Tierney, R. J., & Pearson, P. D. (1994). Learning to learn from text: A framework for improving classroom practice. In R. B. Ruddell, M. R. Ruddell, & H. Singer (Eds.), *Theoretical models and processes of reading* (pp. 496–513). Newark, DE: International Reading Association.

Tierney, R. J., & Pearson, P. D. (1992). Learning to learn from text: A framework for improving classroom practice. In E. K. Dishner, T. W. Bean, J. E. Readence, & D. W. Moore (Eds.), *Reading in the content areas: Improving classroom instruction.* Dubuque, IA: Kendall/Hunt.

Tovani, C. (2000). *I read it, but I don't get it: Comprehension strategies for adolescent readers.* Portland, ME: Stenhouse.

Venezky, R. L. (2000). The origins of the present-day chasm between adult literacy needs and school literacy instruction. *Scientific Studies of Reading, 4,* 19–39.

Vockell, E. L. (1995). Educational psychology: A practical approach. Retrieved September 21, 2004, from http://education.calumet.purdue.edu/vockell/EPsyBook

Vygotsky, L. (1986). *Thought and language.* Boston: MIT Press.

Wallis, C. (2006). The multitasking generation. *Time, 167,* 48–55.

Walpole, S. (1998). Changing texts, changing thinking: Comprehension demands of new science textbooks. *The Reading Teacher, 52,* 358–369.

Wilhelm, J. D. (2001). *Improving comprehension with think-aloud strategies.* New York: Scholastic.

Wilhelm, J. D. (2002). *Action strategies for deepening comprehension.* New York: Scholastic.

Wurman, R. S., Leifer, L., Sume, S., & Whitehouse, K. (2000). *Information anxiety 2.* New York: Que.

Zook, K. B., & Maier, J. M. (1994). Systematic analysis of variables that contribute to the formation of analogical misconceptions. *Journal of Educational Psychology, 86*(4), 589–600.

Children's Books Cited

Berger, M. (1993). *Animals in hiding.* New York: Newbridge.

Canizares, S., & Chessen, B. (1998). *From egg to robin.* New York: Scholastic.

Cole, S. (2000). *Manatees and dugongs.* Bothell, WA: Wright Group.

Cowley, J. (2005). *Chameleon, chameleon.* New York: Scholastic.

Farmer, J. (2004). *Pumpkins.* Watertown, MA: Charlesbridge Publishing.

Fehlner, P. (1999). *Hiding in plain sight.* New York: Harcourt Brace & Co.

Folsom, M., & Elting, M. (1980). *Q is for duck.* New York: Houghton Mifflin.

Freeman, M. (1998). *The wetlands.* New York: Newbridge.

Hayes, S. (1996). The cost of child labor. *Scholastic News.*

Heller, R. (1999). *Chickens aren't the only ones.* New York: Grosset & Dunlap.

Jenkins, M. (1999). *The emperor's egg.* Cambridge, MA: Candlewick Press.

Jenkins, M. (2001). *Chameleons are cool.* Cambridge, MA: Candlewick Press.

Most, B. (1990). *Dinosaur cousins.* New York: Harcourt Brace.

Most, B. (1995). *How big were the dinosaurs?* New York: Harcourt Brace.

Noonan, D. (1994). *Bird beaks.* Bothell, WA: Wright Group.

Shirley, A. (1993). *Eggs and baby birds.* Bothell, WA: Wright Group.

Wells, R. E. (1993). *Is a blue whale the biggest thing there is?* Morton Grove, IL: Albert Whitman & Company.

Wells, R. E. (1996). *How do you lift a lion?* Morton Grove, IL: Albert Whitman & Company.

Wells, R. E. (1999). *What's smaller than a pygmy shrew?* Morton Grove, IL: Albert Whitman & Company.

Index